CW00811959

Be My Guest

The Georgian recipe *for* cooking success

Anna Saldadze & David Gigauri

sulakauri
PUBLISHING

"Every Georgian dish is a Poem"

Alexander Pushkin

Contents

Preface   5

Every Recipe is a Signature `
  by Keti Bakradze   6

Until you have seen Georgia you have seen nothing...
  by John Steinbeck   8

Salome Andronikov   20

Prince and Princess Peter Bagration   38

George Balanchine   40

Gogi Is the Gimmick at Larue
  by Murray Robinson   78

The Mdivanis   90

George Papashvily   94

Tamara Toumanova   110

Prince Nicholas Toumanoff   120

How I discovered Tamadism
  by Michel Eltchaninoff   122

Preface

From the times of the Golden Fleece right up to the digital age Georgia has always been a known leader in the arts of hospitality, food and wine. Indeed 'Georgian hospitality' with its highly codified 'supra' (a feast covering the entire table) is the axis and inner sanctum of the nation's talent for charming its guests and invaders (of which there were many). Indeed some have suggested this may be the secret to the nation's very existence today - food as a tool of cultural survival in which the enemy is systematically transformed into a friend.

It can be no coincidence that the nation also gave birth to viniculture seven thousand years ago, developing a similarly rich and diverse indigenous cuisine to accompany its evolving culture of the feast.

Due to the turbulent fate of the country (Georgia is historically one of the most invaded nations on earth) many times Georgians have found themselves living away from their homeland. But for most this never prevented the indulgence of their table DNA, nor a continuing tradition of hospitality in their adopted lands. Not only an excellent means of adapting to environment and cementing friendship, it helped keep their personal identity alive. It is no surprise that many entered the hospitality industry - such as the celebrity restaurateur Gogi Tchitchinadze; Nicholas Eristoff (Eristavi) the man behind Eristoff vodka; and Alexander Tarsaidze who introduced Caucasian Shashlik to the Waldorf-Astoria group of hotels in New York. For them food is a universal language, which with aid of a few glasses of Saperavi red or a personalised cocktail, can make the barriers fall. A good Georgian 'tamada' (toast maker) will employ the combined talents of story-telling, flattery and full-on charm to make guests quickly forget their differences, open up and remember again the life-enhancing qualities that a meal in its essence provides. See the semi-fictional essay *'How I discovered Tamadism'* by Michel Eltchaninoff on page 122.

This book spells out the favourite recipes of Georgia's more exceptional expatriates, along with their stories, and in their language (hence the occasional imperfections in the English). While they achieved fame and success in different fields, one has to remember that their accomplishments were always matched back at home by skills in the kitchen or at the table - for which they were equally remembered by their guests. For instance Prince Bagration, the illustrious general of the Napoleonic Wars, is famous for throwing sumptuous dinners for his troops, regardless of whether the battle was won or lost. George Balanchine, the founder of the New York City Ballet, arrived in America on a mission to make the entire continent fall in love with him and coriander. He surely succeeded with the first and probably the second.

The recipes themselves are either authentically Georgian; improvised versions of the originals; or personal dedications to Georgians themselves - like Lobster à la Bagration by the 'King of Chefs and Chef of Kings,' Marie-Antoine (Antonin) Carême.

But in truth this national epicurism stems from a simple fact, an instinctive love of people and the dramas they create. The Georgian table has always served as a superb domestic theatre for portrayals of great heroism, romanticism or foolishness, related in the safety of laughing faces, presided over by the delicious aromas of food.

Anna Saldadze and David Gigauri

Every recipe is a signature

George Balanchine, Prince Bagration, Salome Andronikov... every Georgian has undoubtedly heard these names, admired their achievements and felt a small twinge of pride knowing they hailed from their homeland. Shooting stars, glowing somewhere over the rainbow, I always asked myself what kind of people they might have been, what were their passions? What were their fears? Discovering their recipes gave me a unique opportunity to get an exclusive insight into their personalities, as cooking, after all, is a very individual and private matter. It is all about you and your relationship with others, your taste, but also your appreciation of the things that surround you. Like body language, it is something unique, it's one's personal signature.

It was a great privilege and pleasure for me to work with their recipes. Even if you do not know that Tamara Toumanova was one of the greatest ballerinas of her generation, when you read her recipes you sense a very rigorous and demanding person, for whom everything is about physical performance, well-being and efficiency.

With Balanchine, it is all about generosity, passion and friendship. Whether it's the Fast Soup he used to prepare for himself and his corps de ballet during long rehearsals, or Easter Paska and Koulichi, they all intended to gather people together around some common cause. Like a pointillist artist placing dots of different colours one next to another in order to create a picture, Balanchine mixes his Georgian influences with all the others gained throughout his adventurous life in Russia, France, Monaco and the United States.

Next to these artists of perfection, it was almost touching to see George Papashvily writing about very traditional Georgian dishes and using his local variations of them, the ones he inherited directly from his family. That is where I realised what it must have meant to him, as an immigrant thousands of miles away from home to cook exactly the same recipes as his relatives were doing in his little village. This gesture goes far beyond the simple act of cooking - it is an act of memory.

As a professional cook, I tried to interpret these intentions and make them visually complementary – with one exception, however: Lobster à la Bagration by Antonin Carême. Since its creation it was always considered more than a dish, rather a culinary work of art. For me it has more to do with symbolism than with a mere recipe for a lobster. That is why I allowed myself to leave it as such, as a representation, as part of imagination, as a legend or a tale of what is woven so deep into Georgian souls.

Keti Bakradze,
Head chef, "The Dining Room"
Tbilisi, Georgia

Until you have seen Georgia you have seen nothing...

In order to put all these culinary experiences of Georgians abroad into context, it is worth noting the reverse - the gastronomic observations of foreigners in Georgia. A fine example of this is a report by the Nobel and Pulitzer Prize winning author John Steinbeck and pioneer of photo-journalism Robert Capa, who visited Georgia together in 1947.

"Wherever we had been in Russia, in Moscow, in the Ukraine, in Stalingrad, the magical name of Georgia came up constantly. People who had never been there, and who possibly never could go there, spoke of Georgia with a kind of longing and a great admiration. They spoke of Georgians as supermen, as great drinkers, great dancers, great musicians, great workers and lovers. And they spoke of the country in the Caucasus and around the Black Sea as a kind of second heaven. Indeed, we began to believe that most Russians hope that if they live good and virtuous lives, they will not go to heaven, but to Georgia, when they die."

These were their first impressions of Georgia before they actually reached the country. They travelled to the then Soviet Union for New York Herald Tribune and their account is published in the book 'A Russian Journal' (1948).

"It is a magical place, Georgia, and it becomes dream-like the moment you have left it. And the people are magic people. It is true that they have one of the richest

"If one tried to describe Georgia using one single word, the right word would definitely be 'hospitality'."

John Steinbeck

and most beautiful countries in the world and they live up to it. And we understood thoroughly now why Russians had always said to us, "Until you have seen Georgia you have seen nothing."

Naturally, a prominent place in their account was assigned to Georgian food and Supra traditions.

"...we stopped at little houses to visit. And they had their gardens and their orchards around them. And in every place we ate a handful of hazelnuts or some country cheese and fresh black bread; a pear just picked from the tree over the house, or a bunch of grapes. We seemed to be eating constantly, and we could not refuse. And we tasted Georgian vodka, which we do not recommend to anyone, for it has a fuse in its tail. It is veritable rocket of a drink, and our stomachs just couldn't take it. Actually it is not vodka at all, but what we used to call grappa, that is distilled wine. It was much too violent for us.

When our stomachs were beginning to bulge with food, the manager of the farm caught up with us. He was a tall, straight, square man, in a partisan uniform and a stiff cap. He asked us to stop by at his house for a bite to eat, God help us! We explained, through Chmarsky and another interpreter, that about one more bite to eat and we would explode. It was returned to us that it was only a token bite, and that he would take it as great courtesy if we would visit his house and have a glass of wine with him.

We had just begun to believe that the Soviet secret weapon, toward guests at least, is food. But we surely could not refuse to have a bite to eat and a glass of wine. And so we went with him to his house, a neat little house on a hill...

Two handsome girls came out of the house with jugs of water. They poured it over our hands, we washed our faces and hands. The girls held out white towels embroidered in red for us to dry ourselves.

And then we were invited to step into the house. Through a hallway we went, and into a large room. The room was hung with woven materials in brilliant colors; some of the designs reminded us of Indian blanketry. The floor was covered with a kind of matting, rather like Mexican petate. It was the vision of the table that nearly killed us. It was about fourteen feet long, and it was loaded with food, and there were about twenty guests. I think it is the only meal or dinner we ever attended where fried chicken was an hors d'oeuvre, and where each hors d'oeuvre was half a chicken. It went from there to a cold boiled chicken over which was poured a cold green sauce, delicious with spices and sour cream. And then there were cheese sticks and tomato salads and Georgian pickles. And then there was a savory stew of lamb, with a thick sauce. And then there was a kind of fried country cheese. There were loaves of flat Georgian rye bread piled up like poker chips, and the center of the table was loaded with fruit, with grapes, and pears, and apples. And the frightful thing about it was that

everything was delicious. The flavors were all new, and we wanted to taste all of them. And were nearly dying of overeating. Capa, who prides himself on a thirty-two-inch waist, and who will not let out his belt, no matter what happens, was getting a puffed look under the chin, and his eyes were slightly popped and bloodshot. And I felt that if I could just go two or three days without eating anything, I might return to normal...

We were introduced to the twenty guests, and we sat down. And here our problem began. If we did not eat, we were urged to eat, and if we did eat, our plates were replenished instantly. And meanwhile the decanters of local wine were passed, and it was a delicious wine, light and full of flavor, and it probably saved our lives. After a few glasses of wine our host stood up, and his wife came from the kitchen and stood beside him, a handsome black-eyed woman with a strong face. The manager drank our health, and drank the health of the United States. And then he appointed his best friend table-master, and this, we were told, is an old Georgian country custom, that the host appoints his friend the master of speeches. And from then on no toast may be made by anyone at the table. If someone wishes to propose a toast, he must pass the word to the table-master, who is usually chosen because of his ability to make speeches. Then the toast is made by the table-master. This saves the guests a great deal of speaking.

The new table-master made quite a long speech. And it must be remembered that even a short speech was long the way it had to be here, for every sentence had to be translated from Georgian to Russian, and from Russian to English. And God knows what ideas were lost or confused on the way, particularly as this dinner progressed...

Since we were foreigners and could not pass a written note to the table-master, we were permitted to answer his toast. And we proposed a toast to the abolishment of curtains of all kinds – of iron curtains, and nylon curtains, and political curtains, and curtains of falsehood, and curtains of superstition. We suggested that curtains were prelude to war, and that if war should come it could be for only one of two reasons – either through stupidity, or through intent, and if it was through intent on the part of any leaders, then those leaders should be removed, and if it was through stupidity, then the causes should be more closely inspected. And we proposed that since no one, not even the most stupid and belligerent of men, could imagine that a modern war could be won by anyone, then any leader on any side who seriously proposed war should be hunted down as an insane criminal and taken out of circulation. Capa has seen a great deal of war, and I have seen a little, and both of us feel very strongly on the subject.

At the end of our toast the wine fairly leaped from the decanters, and everyone at the table stood up, and everyone insisted on touching his glass to the glass of everyone else at the table. And there was the intimate Georgian toast. Each man holding a

"In every place we ate a handful of hazelnuts or some country cheese and fresh black bread; a pear just picked from the tree over the house, or a bunch of grapes. We seemed to be eating constantly, and we could not refuse."

John Steinbeck

glass links his arm with his neighbor's arm and drinks from his own glass. The women leaned from the kitchen, and around the entranceway the neighbors had gathered, and the wine decanters were passed out to them.

The Georgians we met are like Welsh. In any group of, say, ten men, there would be at least seven fine voices. And at this table now the singing broke out, magnificent choral singing. They sang the songs of the Georgian shepherds of the mountains, and the old fighting songs. And the voices were so good, and the chorus was so good, that they seemed to be almost professional group, and they were not. And then the tempo quickened, and two men took chairs, and turned them over their knees, and used them for drums, and the dancing started. The women came out of the kitchen and danced, and the men leaped up from the table and danced. And the music was the chorus of male voices, and the patted chair bottoms, and the clapping of hands.

It was magnificent dance music. Sometimes a man would dance alone, and sometimes a woman alone, and sometimes they danced together, in formal quick steps, traditional dances of Georgia. And this is how it was when we stopped for just a bite to eat and a glass of wine in a Georgian farmhouse. We had to tear ourselves away...

We were taking the train to Tiflis that night, and we were supposed to go to the theater before train time. And so heavy were we with fatigue, and food, and wine, and impressions, that the theater left not very much mark on us. It was Oedipus Rex played in Georgian, and our eyes were barely open enough to see that Oedipus was a handsome man with a flashing gold tooth, and that his red wig was magnificently red... The audience spent half its time turning and looking at us, the visiting Americans. We were only a little less rare than visiting Martians here, and we couldn't have appeared to advantage, for we were half asleep. Our host led us out of the theater, and pushed us into a car, and got us up the stairs of the train, and we were like sleepwalkers... We fell into our berths and went to sleep almost immediately.

In these terrific Georgians we had met more than our match. They could out-eat us, out-drink us, out-dance us, out-sing us. They had the fierce gaiety of the Italians, and the physical energy of the Burgundians. Everything they did was done with flair. They were quite different from Russians we had met, and it is easy to see why they are so admired by the citizens of the Soviet republics.

Their energy not only survives but fattens on a tropical climate. And nothing can break their individuality or their spirit. That has been tried for so many centuries by invaders, by czarist armies, by despots, by the little local nobility. Everything has struck at their spirit and nothing had succeeded in making a dent in it.

Our train got into Tiflis about eleven o'clock, and we slept until just little before that time, and struggled into our clothes, and went to our hotel, and slept some more. And we did not eat, not even a cup of tea did we have, for there was one more thing we had to do before we flew back to Moscow the next morning. That night we were to be given a party by the intellectuals and the artists of Tiflis. It was not that we seemed to be eating practically all the time – we were.

Just as the body can become flooded, and inattentive to rich food and wines, so that the perception of spices and vintages disappears, so can a mind become drowned with impressions, overwhelmed with scenes, imperceptive of colors and movements. And we were suffering both from overeating, overdrinking, and overseeing. It is said that in a foreign country impressions are sharp and accurate for a month, and then they become blurred, and the reactions are not accurate again for five years, so that one should stay either one month or five years in a country.

We had the feeling that we were not seeing things sharply any more. And we had a certain terror of the dinner of the intellectuals of Georgia that night. We were so tired, and we did not want to hear speeches, particularly intellectual speeches. We did not want to think about art, or politics, or economics, or international relations, and particularly we did not want to eat or drink. We wanted mainly just to go to bed and sleep until plane time. But the Georgians had been so kind to us, and so pleasant, that we knew that we had to go to this dinner. It was the one formal thing they had asked us to do. And we should have trusted the Georgians and their national genius more, because the dinner did not turn out at all like what we had suspected it might.

Our clothes were in outrageous condition. We hadn't brought very many, you can't when you fly, and our trousers hadn't been pressed since we had entered the Soviet Union. And little accidents of food were upon our coats. Our shirts were clean but badly ironed. We were far from beautiful examples of the overdressed America. But Capa washed his hair, and that had to do for both of us. We sponged the more removable spots from clothes, and put on clean shirts, and we were ready.

They took us in the funicular railway straight up the cliff to the great restaurant at the top which overlooks the whole of the valley. It was evening when we went up, and the city was lighted below us. And the evening sky was golden behind the black Caucasus peaks.

It was a big party. The table seemed about a mile long. It was set for about eighty people, for the dancers of Georgia were there, and the singers, and the composers and the makers of motion pictures; and the poets and the novelists. The table was covered with flowers and beautifully decorated and set, and the city was like strings of diamonds below the cliff. There were many handsome women singers and dancers.

The dinner started, as all such dinners do, with a few stuffy speeches, but the Georgian nature, and the Georgian genius, couldn't tolerate it, and it went to pieces almost immediately. They just are not stuffy people, and they could not contrive to be for very long. Singing broke out, individual singing and group singing. And dancing broke out. And the wine passed. And Capa did his famous kazatzki, which is not graceful, but it

is remarkable that he can do it at all. Perhaps the sleep we had got gave us new life, and perhaps the wine helped a little, for the party went on very late into the night. I recall a Georgian composer who raised his glass, and laughed, and said, "To hell with politics!" I recall trying to do a Georgian dance with a handsome woman who turned out to be the greatest Georgian dancer in the world. I recall group singing in the street finally, and that the militia came to see what the singing was about, and joined the chorus. Mr. Chmarsky was a little gay. He was as strange to Georgia as we were. Language barriers went down, national boundaries went down, and there was no need of translators any more.

We had a wonderful time, and this dinner which we had looked forward to with horror and reluctance turned out to be a magnificent party.

In the dawn we dragged ourselves back to our hotel. There was no purpose in going to bed, for our plane would leave in a very few hours. We were half dead packing our bags, but some way we got to the airport, we will never know how.

John Steinbeck
A Russian Journal, 1948

Salome Andronikov

Known as the 'Muse of the Silver Age' Salome was a prominent socialite in the literary and artistic salons of pre-revolutionary St. Petersburg. She became an inspiration and subject for some of the greatest artists and poets of the age, including Konstantin Somov, Kuzma Petrov-Vodkin, Savelii Sorine, Zinaida Serebriakova, Boris Grigoriev, Sergey Chekhonin, Osip Mandelstam, Anna Akhmatova, Marina Tsvetaeva.

"All my life I believed myself to be a muse, but in the end turned out to be merely a cook"

Salome Andronikov (Andronikashvili)

"I am neither a professional cook nor a scientific expert on cookery. But when after the war I returned to (England) and found conditions so radically changed that there was no question of resuming the old way of life, with servants doing all the work for me, I realized that, whether I liked it or not, I would have to do the cooking myself. This was quite a problem, for I knew literally nothing about it. By now, however, I have become a fairly good cook. I entertain a great deal and all my friends seem to enjoy my dinners."

"Cooking can be more than good fun. It makes you improvise, explore your imagination. It can in every sense be a truly creative act."

Salome Andronikov

Georgian Ratatouille

Georgian Ratatouille

3-4 aubergines
225g or 450g/½ or 1 pound tomatoes
1-2 onions
Parsley, tarragon
Margarine and oil (or oil only)
Seasoning

First method

Peel the aubergines and cut them in rather thick slices. Chop the onions. Cut the tomatoes in half. Chop parsley and tarragon. Keep all the vegetables separate.

Cook the aubergines in boiling salted water for about five minutes. Drain. Fry all the vegetables in turn, including the aubergines, in a mixture of margarine and oil (or oil alone if you prefer it), till they are brown and soft. Season the tomatoes, adding a little sugar.

When all the vegetables are ready, arrange them in layers in a deep dish (aubergines first, then tomatoes, then onions, and aubergines again) and finish cooking in the oven. The longer you cook it – the better it will taste. It can be cooked in advance, and heated up for the desired meal. A ratatouille is always better the next day, whether warmed up or eaten cold.

Second method

When all the vegetables are cut up, you brown the onions only, put everything together into a saucepan, season with pepper, salt and sugar, and cook on a low flame for several hours. Do not add any water: these vegetables usually give out sufficient liquid. But you must watch them: if there is not enough liquid, do add a little water.

Note: If you eat the ratatouille cold, season with oil and vinegar. Usually no additional salt or pepper are required as these were already used in the cooking. Served in this way, the ratatouille makes a delicious hors d'oeuvre.

Chikhertma

Chicken broth
4 good-sized onions
115g/4 ounces butter or margarine
2 eggs
2 tablespoons flour
Salt, pepper, sugar
A little vinegar or lemon juice

If you have a boiled chicken, you can use the stock for an excellent Georgian soup. Chop 4 onions very finely. Cook them gently (it is essential not to let them brown) in at least 115 g/4 oz. of butter or margarine, adding two tablespoonfuls flour. When the onions are thoroughly cooked and very soft, pour a little hot chicken broth over them and slowly bring again to the boil, stirring continuously. Then mix with the rest of the broth and let simmer for another hour.

Just before serving break two egg yolks into a large bowl, and mix with 1-2 teaspoons of sugar. Pour in the hot soup, stirring all the time, add some lemon juice to taste, and serve.

(With any soup [or sauce] containing milk, cream or eggs, lemon juice should be added at the very last moment. Otherwise the soup may curdle.)

Chikhertma

"The jewel of the evening, as always, was Salome Andronikov –
not a writer, not a poet, not an actress, not a dancer and not a
singer. A complete *naught*. But she was recognised as the most
interesting woman in our circle... "

Nadezhda Tef
Russian humourist write

In 1965, the poet Anna Akhmatova was visiting her old friend Salome Andronikov in England.

– Your cooking has come a long way Salome! – Akhmatova noted in amazement, while sampling some of her exquisite delicacies – not so long ago you were unable to brew a cup of tea!

– I had to learn how to cook, – Salome smiled, – now that I am knocking on a bit, I have nothing else left to attract men!

Aubergine Caviar

Blood-coloured drunkenness of pomegranates in heat
Summons the females for debauchery
Dark outcry increased in time and volume
Of promiscuous reflections of the night-time

Salome – tigress all in flames
Beside wild shrub somewhere in the garden
Lovesummonning, numbambering
And kissing lifeless lips of the deceased

Grigol Robakidze
Translated into English by Kote Gogolashvili

Fried Aubergines

Aubergine Caviar

2-3 aubergines
Onion
2-3 tomatoes
Parsley, salt, pepper
Oil, vinegar

Do not peel the aubergines. Put them whole into the oven and bake them till quite soft. When cooled, the skin will come away quite easily. Chop them, or crush with a fork. Add some finely chopped raw onion and some finely chopped parsley, and season as any other salad, with salt, pepper, oil and vinegar.

Another method is to add to the crushed aubergines some onion previously fried in oil and one or two tomatoes. Mix well, season, and cook for few minutes. Serve cold.

Fried Aubergines

Aubergines
Flour
Oil
Seasoning

Peel the aubergines and cut them lengthways into thin slices. Add salt and let them stand for about an hour. Drain. Season with pepper and roll in flour. Fry in very hot oil until crisp, and serve immediately. The frying must be done at the last moment, but all the preparation can of course be carried out in advance.

Walnut Sauce "Satzivi"

Cold turkey or chicken in walnut sauce

1 roasting chicken
450g/1 pound walnuts
1 cup of vinegar
1 cup red or white wine
Some parsley
25g/1 ounce margarine
1 small strong red pimento
Salt, pepper

Cut the bird into pieces and fry with some finely chopped onion. Clean 450g/1 lb of walnuts and chop them (do not grate or pound them, as this would be too fine). Put them into a saucepan with vinegar and wine, a little margarine and seasoning, and bring to the boil.

Put the chicken pieces into a casserole, pour the sauce over them, add some chopped parsley and a piece of chopped strong red pimento, cover with a lid and let it stew slowly till the bird is cooked. The dish is always eaten cold.

Walnut Sauce "Baje"

Walnuts (450g/1 pound of unshelled equals 225g/½ pound of shelled walnuts)
Some vinegar, diluted
Salt, pepper

Pound or grate some walnuts. Moisten them with vinegar diluted with water. It should have the consistency of a thick gritty paste. Season with salt and a little pepper. Mix well and serve with trout or salmon, hot or cold.

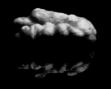
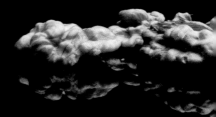

The Russian journalist, writer, and poet, Larissa Vasilieva would always depict Salome as very much the epitome of contemporary style and grace.

"We sat at a large table in her elongated kitchen having dinner. As always, she would impress with her culinary talent. Salome is tall, slender, with short curly grey hair, made up cheeks and lips, wearing a long formal dress.

– I always change into a long dress for supper, regardless of whether I have guests or not – said Salome – it's a habit."

This recipe is almost identical to the one the Bolshoi ballerina Maya Plisetskaya arranged to have published in American Vogue.

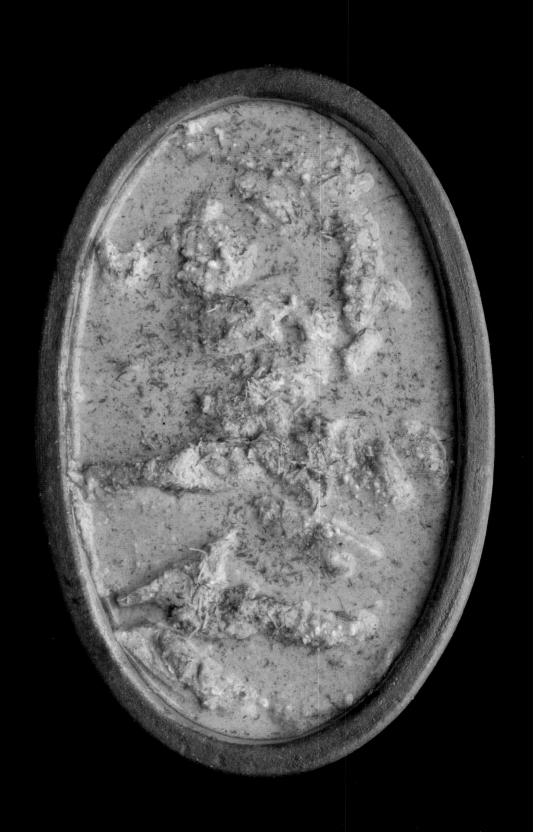

Walnut Sauce "Baje"

Walnut Sauce "Baje"

Prince and Princess Peter Bagration

Descendent of the Georgian royal family, hero of the Napoleonic Wars, legendary military commander, General Bagration is also featured in Leo Tolstoy's *War and Peace*.

"Had there been no Bagration, it would have been necessary to invent him", as Tolstoy's character Shinshin put it, in a parody of Voltaire's famous phrase.

Bagration's reputation as a connoisseur of the good life is well documented. The prince enjoyed taking time off from the battlefield to return to his palace in St. Petersburg where he and his wife, Princess Katerina, often invited three or four hundred guests to an eight course meal, "service à la Russe".

The same refined culinary tradition was then continued in France, where the "King of Chefs, and the Chef of Kings" Marie-Antoine Carême ran the kitchen of the Bagration household. In late 1819, Carême created Lobster à la Bagration, dedicated to Princess Katerina Bagration.

Lobster à la Bagration

4 servings
500g/1 pound 2 ounces turnips
500g/1 pound 2 ounces carrots
250g/9 ounces peas
500g/1 pound 2 ounces green beans
1 to 2 litres of Château La Baronne
4 lobsters
Brawn, parsley, "Hermitage" mayonnaise, chervil, tarragon

Cook the vegetables and mix them with the brawn. Fill some small, triangular moulds with this mixture. Remove them once the mixture has set and place the triangles upright in the middle of a base. Cook the lobsters in a white wine and leave them to cool. Cut the tails into small medallions and lightly glaze them in a little brawn. Place them in a crown arrangement around the vegetables and decorate using the shells, claws and small bouquets of fresh herbs. Serve the "Hermitage" mayonnaise with the chives, chervil and tarragon.

"This delicacy isn't a mere dish: it is a true work of art!"

Antonius Moonen
Petit Breviaire du Snobisme

George Balanchine

The "Father of American Ballet" George Balanchine (Balanchivadze), was the co-founder, artistic director and choreographer of the New York City Ballet. He also founded the School of American Ballet at Lincoln Center for the Performing Arts in New York City. His ballets include *The Nutcracker*, *Swan Lake*, *Jewels* amongst 400 other works. He was also a pioneer choreographer for Broadway musicals and Hollywood films, including *The Goldwyn Follies*, *On Your Toes*, *The Ziegfeld Follies*.

"Any good artist leaves behind works of value when he dies. When a great artist dies, he leaves an entire landscape transformed. George Balanchine, the protean choreographer, left his imprint virtually everywhere in dance... Balanchine style may be evolving into a lingua franca for ballet in the 21st century — a common language of dance spoken by everybody, everywhere. Choreography, Balanchine suggested, wasn't a lofty art but a craft like that of a cabinetmaker or a chef turning out his sauces and soufflés."

Christopher Porterfield, *Balancing Balanchine*
Time Magazine, 2004

"I don't care about past. And future – I wouldn't know what it is.
To me, today is everything."
George Balanchine

"Of all our friends, George Balanchine was in the highest sense a bon vivant. The sensual pleasure he found in food and wine was surpassed only by the delight he took in shaping the bodies of his magnificently trained dancers to the myriad designs of his ballets.

The great choreographer said of himself, quoting the Russian poet Vladimir Mayakovsky: 'I'm "not a man, but a cloud in trousers".' Certainly this Magician, this Prospero of the Dance, was as elusive, as immaterial, and as ever-changing as a cloud. Unlike the wise cat in the Russian legend who spoke in verse when he turned to the left and in prose when he turned to the right, Balanchine, no matter which way he turned, always spoke his personal poetry... Silent and pensive at times, he was also capable of suddenly releasing a devastating avalanche of irony, wit, opinion (prejudiced and otherwise), paradox, and above all, flights of fancy open to as many interpretations as his ballets.

...His daily life, like ballet itself, was one of constant motion. When he was not creating ballets or rehearsing his dancers, he was apt to be gardening, puttering about the house, or cooking. It was a very moving experience to watch the creator of *Serenade* and *Agon*, *Concerto Barocco*, and *The Four Temperaments* peel carrots and slice potatoes with the same intensity he gave to his choreography. To all of his activities he brought a confident, uninterrupted flow of ideas and an intense concentration, the concentration of genius that we have witnessed in only three people: Stravinsky, Picasso and Balanchine himself."

Arthur Gold and Robert Fizdale
Food for Good Living

Gogli-Mogli

3 servings
6 egg yolks
6 tablespoons sugar
½ teaspoon vanilla

Put all the ingredients in the top of a double boiler over simmering water. Beating continuously, heat until light, fluffy, and somewhat thick. Pour into a bowl or wine glasses and chill.

"At bedtime my brother, my sister, and I sat around Mama in a semicircle. She had a glass of gogli-mogli and a spoon. While she fed one, the other two watched to see who got the biggest spoonful. We were like little birds in a nest fed by the mama bird." – Balanchines "sweetest" childhood memories would emerge at the taste of this scrumptious snack.

Kasha

"While he showed us how to prepare kasha, George told us about the first meal he ever cooked. It was for Diaghilev and dancers of the Ballet Russes in Monte Carlo. Balanchine, only twenty, was already a choreographer for the legendary ballet company. His first menu was an ambitious one.

'I made fillet of sole – came out mushy; chicken cutlets – mushy; soufflé – mushy. Everything looked like kasha; was awful!'

Diaghilev, always elegant, turned as he left the table, where most of the food remained uneaten, and, bowing courteously to each platter in turn, said, 'Kasha number one, kasha number two, kasha number three, and thank you, George!'"

Arthur Gold and Robert Fizdale
Food for Good Living

Kasha

4-5 servings
150g/1 cup finely chopped onions
2 tablespoons butter
1 egg, lightly beaten
245g/1½ cups whole-grain buckwheat groats
(it is essential that you use whole-grain buckwheat)
565ml/2 cups beef broth
Salt and freshly ground pepper to taste
Preheat the oven to 180°C/350°F

Sauté the onions in the butter over medium heat, stirring often, until they are golden brown. Reserve. Put the buckwheat groats in a heavy frying pan over medium heat with no fat in the pan. Stir constantly for a few minutes until the groats are toasted and give off a nutty aroma. Add the beaten egg and stir until every grain is coated.

Bring the broth to a boil. Pour just enough of it into the pan to cover the groats. Bring the broth back to a boil. Transfer the pan to the oven.

From time to time, add more boiling broth (or water) to keep the groats covered. When a crust forms on top, remove the skillet from the oven and stir, scraping the bottom and turning the crust under. Taste the kasha after 20 minutes. It should have the constituency of rice cooked al dente. From now on, add just enough broth to keep the kasha from sticking. Dry it in the oven until a crust forms two or three more times, turning the crust under each time. (Cooking time: approximately 1 hour.) Remove from the oven, add salt and pepper and stir in the sautéed onions. Return to the oven until a final crust is formed.

Tip: For a delicious salad, mix cold leftover kasha with chopped red or green pepper and toss with vinaigrette.

Salade Niçoise à la Balanchine

Vinaigrette

145ml/½ cup lemon juice
215ml/¾ cup extra-virgin olive oil
1 medium shallot, minced
1 tablespoon minced fresh thyme leaves
2 tablespoons minced fresh basil leaves
2 teaspoons minced fresh oregano leaves
1 teaspoon Dijon mustard
Salt and freshly ground black pepper

Salad

2 grilled tuna steaks* or 2-3 cans of tuna
6 hard-boiled eggs
10 small new red potatoes
Salt and freshly ground black pepper
2 medium heads Boston lettuce or butter
lettuce
3 small ripe tomatoes
1 small red onion
225g/1½ cups green beans
40g/¼ cup niçoise olives
2 tablespoons capers, rinsed and/
or several anchovies (optional)

*Marinate tuna steaks in a little olive oil for an hour. Heat a large skillet on medium high heat, or place on a hot grill. Cook the steaks 2 to 3 minutes on each side until cooked through.

1 Whisk lemon juice, oil, shallot, thyme, basil, oregano, and mustard in a medium bowl; season to taste with salt and pepper and set aside.

2 Bring potatoes and 4 quarts cold water to boil in a large pot. Add 1 tablespoon salt and cook until potatoes are tender, 5 to 8 minutes. Transfer potatoes to a medium bowl with a slotted spoon (do not discard boiling water). Toss warm potatoes with ¼ cup vinaigrette; set aside.

3 While potatoes are cooking, toss lettuce with ¼ cup vinaigrette in large bowl until coated. Arrange bed of lettuce on a serving platter. Cut tuna into 1cm/½-inch thick slices, coat with vinaigrette. Mound tuna in centre of lettuce. Toss tomatoes, red onion, 3 tablespoons vinaigrette, and salt and pepper to taste in bowl; arrange tomato-onion mixture on the lettuce bed. Arrange reserved potatoes in a mound at edge of lettuce bed.

4 Return water to boil; add 1 tablespoon salt and green beans. Cook until tender but crisp, 3 to 5 minutes. Drain beans, transfer to reserved ice water, and let stand until just cool, about 30 seconds; dry beans well. Toss beans, 3 tablespoons vinaigrette, and salt and pepper to taste; arrange in a mound at edge of lettuce bed.

5 Arrange hard boiled eggs, olives and anchovies (if using) in mounds on the lettuce bed. Drizzle eggs with remaining 2 tablespoons dressing, sprinkle entire salad with capers (if using), and serve immediately.

Salade Niçoise à la Balanchine

"Reminiscing about Diaghilev days that evening at dinner, one of the guests, a ballerina, was trying to place the year in which her husband first danced a leading role in one of Balanchine's ballets.

'It is the year your husband jumped into bed with Diaghilev,' said Balanchine.

'He never jumped into bed with Diaghilev,' said the indignant ballerina, 'and besides….if he did…it was the year after.'

Balanchine smiled enigmatically, heaped a second serving onto every plate and, in a triumphant stage whisper, said to us, 'It was the year before; and, anyway, he never could jump!'"

Arthur Gold and Robert Fizdale
Food for Good Living

Georgian Coriander sauce

2 cups chopped coriander
½ cup chopped fresh herbs (parsley, dill, basil or tarragon)
½ cup chopped scallions
½ cup walnuts
2 or more cloves garlic, finely chopped
6 cooked prunes, pitted and chopped
4 tablespoons lemon juice or vinegar
1 cup walnut oil or more if needed
Salt, pepper, and cayenne pepper to taste

In a mortar or wooden bowl, mash together the herbs, walnuts, garlic, and prunes. Stir in the lemon juice, oil, and seasoning.

"In the Caucasus, coriander sauce is ever-present. It is served with hors d'oeuvres of cold sautéed eggplant slices and thickly sliced ripe tomatoes, and in kidney-bean and potato salads. It is used on fish, roast meat, chicken, and 'the best of all', Balanchine used to say, 'on sliced leftover white meat of turkey or any other nice leftovers.'"

Nice leftovers in coriander sauce were frequently enjoyed by Mr. B., as his friends used to call him, and something he gladly offered to guests.

"A persistent acquaintance of Balanchine's who had been hinting regularly that he would like to be invited to dinner telephoned one morning. George's conversation with him ended: 'What am I doing? Well, as a matter of fact, we're cooking tonight's dinner. You'd like to come? I hope you like leftovers. Yes? You do? Good! Come tomorrow.'"

Arthur Gold and Robert Fizdale
Food for Good Living

Balanchine always felt that shopping for cucumbers was a serious business that required great skill and physical dexterity.

"I watch big, fat ladies fighting to get biggest, fattest cucumbers which are lousy and I stand behind them, like eagle, on my toes. Then, when I see tiny, green, firm young cucumbers, I swoop down and pounce on them and fly home."

Cucumber Pickles

4 litre/gallon jars with tight-fitting lids.
18 pieces of 10 cm/4 inches long cucumbers
Dill, salt

Wash cucumbers and trim off a little bit from each end. The dill must be fresh and aromatic. As the cucumber absorbs the flavour of the dill, old, rotten dill results in old, rotten-tasting cucumbers. The best dill to use is from the garden, picked when the florets are just starting to go to seed. For a 4 litre/gallon jar, three such stalks would be enough, but bought at your grocer four or five stalks will do. Wash the dill thoroughly and break each stalk in three or four pieces.

Use half a cup of kosher (coarse) salt to eight cups (2 litres/1/2 gallon) of water. Bring water and salt to a boil. Layer the jar with cucumbers and dill until you reach the top. Add the boiling salted water. When cool, cap and refrigerate. Forget for four days.

Serve at the festive table where cucumber salad is usually found next to the sturgeon in aspic.

Pickles are best enjoyed with 50/100g of Eristoff Vodka (now part of the Bacardi group). The original recipe, still used today, was developed in 1806 by Prince Eristavi of Georgia's mountainous region, Racha.

Sauerkraut & Tomatoes

1.8 kilos/4 pounds sauerkraut
½ cup oil
15 peppercorns
2 bay leaves
3 tomatoes, peeled and cut in wedges
1 teaspoon onion salt
1 200g/6 ounce can tomato paste.

Drain sauerkraut in a colander, then place in a bowl. Pour boiling water over it; stir and drain. Repeat. The sauerkraut is now ready. Place in a saucepan with oil, peppercorns, and bay leaves. Cook covered, over low heat, until golden brown, about 1 hour, stirring occasionally with a wooden spoon.

Cook tomatoes in a skillet until soft, add onion salt and tomato paste, simmer 5 minutes. Add tomato mixture to sauerkraut, taste and correct seasoning. Simmer covered 1 hour, stirring occasionally. Serves 8.

In a mortar or wooden bowl, mash together the herbs, walnuts, garlic, and prunes. Stir in the lemon juice, oil, and seasoning.

Sauerkraut & Mushrooms

1.8 kilos/2 pound sauerkraut
4 tablespoons oil
4 large dried mushrooms
2 tablespoons oil
1 bay leaf
2 teaspoons seasoned salt
½ teaspoon onion powder
Ground pepper
1 cup sour cream

Soak mushrooms in warm water 30 minutes, changing water twice to eliminate sand. Cook in boiling water to cover until tender, about ¾ hour. Drain, reserving liquid and mince. Sauté minced mushrooms in 2 tablespoons oil with bay leaf, seasoned salt, onion powder and ground pepper. Add minced mushrooms, reserved mushroom liquid and sour cream to sauerkraut. Simmer uncovered 10 minutes. May be served with boiled potatoes or buckwheat kasha. Serves 4-6.

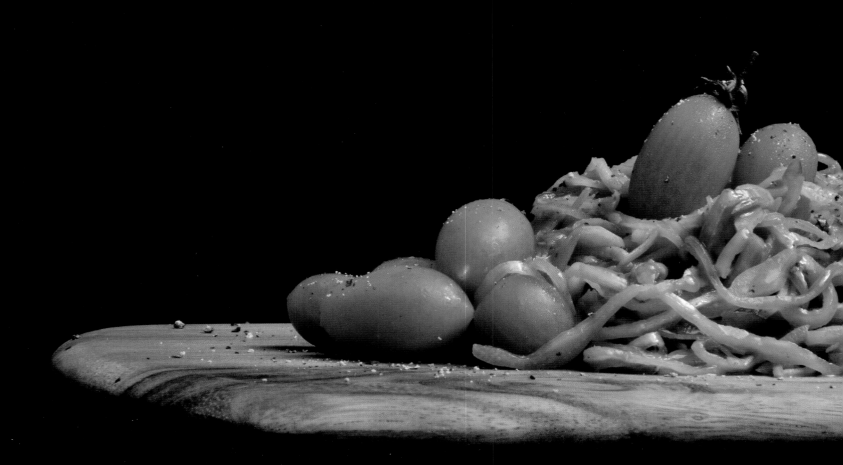

"When we asked George what he would choose if he were on a desert island and could have only one dish, before we could complete the question he answered, "Potatoes! Nah-turally! Nice, excellent, fahntahstic hot boiled potatoes – crunchy, crisp – like sugar." Then after a moment's reflection, he added plaintively, "Could I have a little oil, a little chopped parsley, and a nice cold bottle of Roederer Cristal champagne?"

Arthur Gold and Robert Fizdale
Food for Good Living

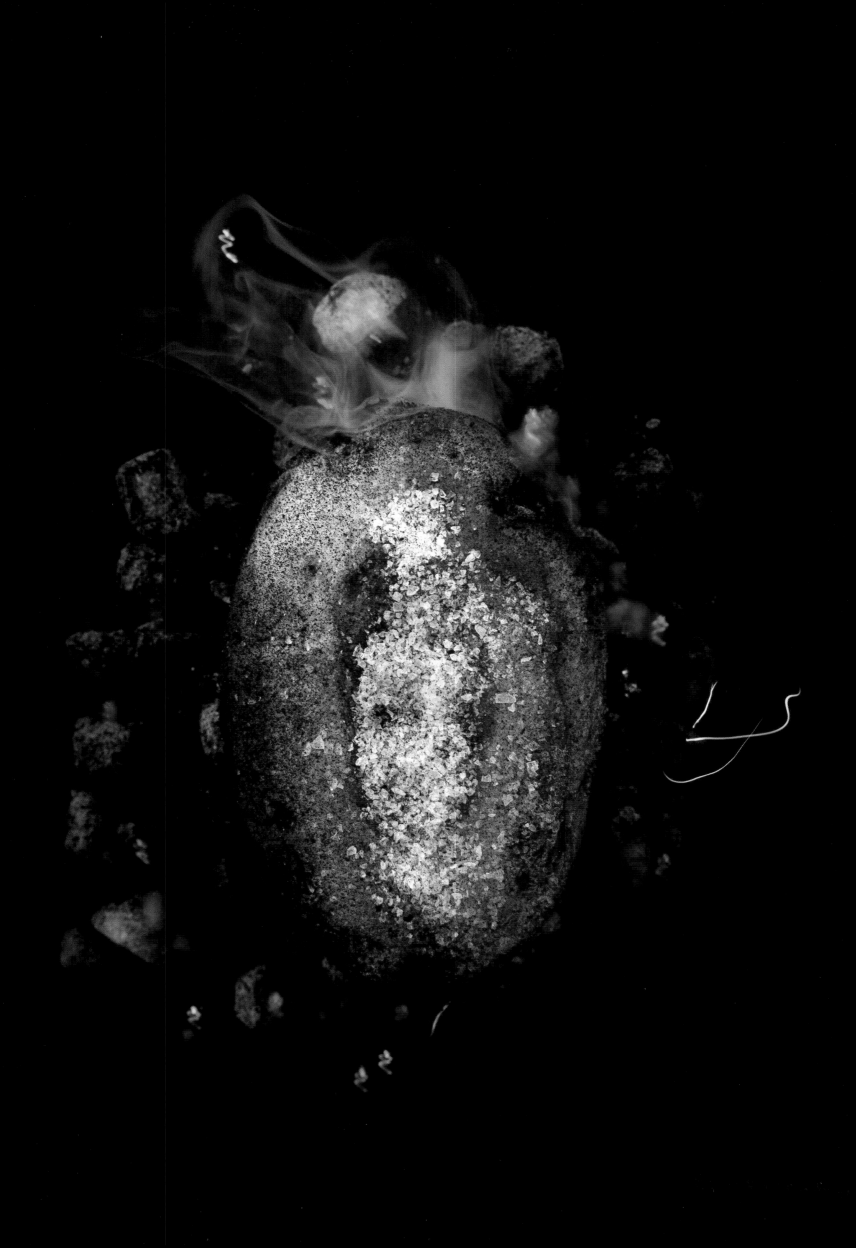

"Since Balanchine usually spent every evening during the ballet season at the New York State Theater, some of his best meals were after theater suppers. One that was unforgettable consisted of borschok, a ruby-red, beef flavored clear consommé. The secret of this soup is baking the beets".

Arthur Gold and Robert Fizdale
Food for Good Living

Fast Soup

2 cans beef bouillon
2 soup cans water
1 potato, peeled and thinly sliced
2 carrots, peeled and thinly sliced
2 parsley roots, peeled and thinly sliced
150g/5 ounces frozen peas
Dill, chopped

Combine bouillon, water, potatoes, carrots and parsley roots in a saucepan. Cook until vegetables are just tender. Add green peas and cook until just soft. Serve with chopped dill. Serves 2.

Borschok à la Balanchine

8-10 servings
8 large or 12 small beets, tops removed
6 cups beef broth, homemade if possible
6 peppercorns
1 bay leaf
1½ teaspoons wine vinegar
1½ teaspoons sugar
Salt and freshly ground pepper to taste
½ cup Madeira
2 lemons, sliced

Wash the beets. Bake them wrapped in aluminum foil for 1 hour, or until they are tender. Cool, peel, and grate them. Put the broth, peppercorns, and bay leaf in a pot and bring to a boil. Add the grated beets, vinegar, and sugar. Stir and simmer for 10 minutes. Strain the soup. Add salt, pepper and the Madeira. Serve in cups, a lemon slice in each.

Cucumber Pickles

His affection for cucumbers extended to his family and friends
"Excellent! When you were smoking, you looked like an old
dill pickle. Now you look like a nice young cucumber!" – was
Balanchine's culinary approval after persuading his friend to
give up smoking.

Fish Dinner for Two

2 tablespoons salad oil
2 tablespoons olive oil
1 pound frozen flounder filets, cut in 8 pieces
Juice ½ lemon
2 bay leaves
½ teaspoon pepper
1 teaspoon salt
2 teaspoons dill weed
¼ teaspoon tarragon
⅛ teaspoon powdered coriander
3 potatoes, peeled, sliced and parboiled
10 cherry tomatoes
½ lemon, sliced

Heat oils in a large skillet, add frozen fish, lemon juice and seasonings. Cook covered over medium heat 8-10 minutes. Add potatoes, tomatoes, and lemon slices and cook until fish is just tender and vegetables are heated through. Serves 2.

Fish Dinner for Two

"Mr B's reputation as a gourmet is such that his prospective hostesses tend to take fright. And this rather delights him, I sometimes think, because his name as a fantastic chef and connoisseur of food assures him an excellent repast wherever he may be invited. It puts his hostesses on their mettle, and as a consequence he is always royally fed.

Under ordinary, everyday conditions (both of us at home for a quiet meal) Fish Dinner for Two, however, is the type meal my husband would be most likely to prepare, especially since he is a devotee of fish."

Tanaquil Le Clercq
The Ballet Book

Wash cheesecloth in boiling water and wring out. Line three large colanders with three thicknesses of the cheesecloth leaving excess around sides. Place cottage cheese in colanders, fold cloth over top, and lay an inverted plate on top of the cloth. Put heavy weights on the plate and place the colanders over bowls to drain at room temperature overnight.

Meanwhile prepare the following ingredients: slit the vanilla beans, scrape out insides and combine with 3 tablespoons sugar; sprinkle almonds with extract; cream butter and 9 cups sugar; beat egg yolks until thick and lemon coloured; add sugar gradually, and continue beating until well combined.

Remove cottage cheese from cheesecloth and, along with the cream cheese, rub through a medium fine sieve into a cauldron. Add the remaining ingredients including the vanilla pods and stir with a wooden spoon to combine.

Half fill a large roasting pan with water and place over two burners. Place a large trivet on the bottom of the roasting pan and set the cauldron on top of the trivet. Heat, stirring often, until the mixture is heated through, about 2 hours. Remove from heat and cool to room temperature. Remove all vanilla pods. Pour mixture into paska molds, flower pots or colanders lined with cheesecloth. Fold cloth over, place weights on top. Set over a bowl, making sure molds are elevated to allow for drainage. Refrigerate three days. Unmold and serve.

"After Orthodox Easter service, Balanchine and his friends would return to his apartment where the traditional three kisses were exchanged, champagne was poured, and everyone gathered around the sumptuous buffet table. It was Balanchine's most elaborate meal of the year. For days before this great feast, his every spare moment between rehearsals and performances was spent rushing home, where with great swiftness and cool dispatch he would work on these intricate dishes".

Arthur Gold and Robert Fizdale
Food for Good Living

Kulichi

5 packages granulated yeast
½ cup warm water
1 tablespoon salt
3 cups sugar
6 cups scalded milk
8 cups sifted flour
1 tablespoon saffron
¼ cup vodka
4 vanilla beans
15 cardamom seeds
¼ cup sugar
2 teaspoon almond extract

2 cups finely chopped blanched almonds
18 egg yolks
1¼ cups sugar
5 cups sweet butter, melted
17 cups sifted flour
1½ cups raisins
½ cup currants
1 egg yolk
1 tablespoon water
Icing:
Juice 1 lemon
1 cup sugar

Dissolve yeast in water. Add salt and 3 cups sugar to milk and stir to dissolve. Cool until lukewarm and stir in dissolved yeast and 8 cups sifted flour. Cover with a towel and allow to rise 1½ hours.

Meanwhile prepare the following for use later on: dissolve saffron in vodka; slit vanilla beans, scrape out insides and combine with crushed cardamom seeds and ¼ cup sugar; combine almond extract with almonds; beat egg yolks until thick and lemon coloured, gradually add 1¼ cups sugar and continue beating until well blended.

Add egg yolk mixture to yeast mixture and stir. Blend in butter and flour alternately, stirring well after each addition. Strain saffron vodka, adding the clear liquid to the yeast mixture. Add remaining ingredients, except egg yolk and water, and blend in thoroughly. The dough will be sticky. Turn out on a lightly floured board and knead 45-60 minutes until the dough is elastic.

Place dough in tall, cylindrical moulds to half fill. Place towel over and allow to rise in a warm place until dough reaches just to top of mould, about 2 ½ hours. Combine egg yolk and water and brush tops of kulichi. Bake at 350°F about 1 hour or until dry when tested with a cake tester. Cool slightly, remove from moulds and allow to cool on racks.

Combine lemon juice and sugar and stir over low heat until sugar melts and the mixture is transparent. Pour over tops of kulichi allowing icing to run down sides. Yields 3 kulichi.

Balanchine had a childlike love of desserts, which he immortalized in his ballet *The Nutcracker*. The decor of the last act of the ballet is indeed a monument to his sweet tooth, a child's paradise of sweets."

Banana Sweet

"One Christmas three very young children were invited to see the first performance of The Nutcracker. Afterwards, with playful yet serious consideration Balanchine showed them the props, seating them on the children's thrones, put them in the reindeer sleigh, and finally led them into and under the skirts of the gigantic Mother Ginger costume.

Happy in their hiding place, the children refused to come out, until Balanchine, like a magician, tugged at a pulley that lifted the costume high into the air exposing the three giggling children. It would be difficult to say who was more delighted, Balanchine or his young guests".

Arthur Gold and Robert Fizdale,
Food for Good Living

Dark ruby Ojaleshi wine is a perfect companion to fruits and sweets. This unique, Western Georgian, grape variety was first cultivated by Princess Salome Dadiani and her husband Prince Achille Murat - grandson of Marshal Joachim Murat and Caroline Bonaparte, sister of Napoleon I of France.

Banana Sweet

Bananas
Butter
Sugar
Lemon juice
White seedless grapes
Apricot jam
Sour cream
Sugar
Slivered almonds

Peel and slice bananas. Fry in butter, sprinkle with sugar and lemon juice. Add grapes and heat through. Transfer to serving dish and spread with apricot jam. Top with sour cream sprinkled with sugar and almonds.

Mr B's Sweet Kasha

1½ cups milk
½ cup Cream of Wheat
2 tablespoons sweet butter
1 tablespoon sugar
Pinch salt
1 225g/8 ounce can Bartlett pears
Apricot jam
Melba sauce
2 ounces slivered almonds, flavoured with ½ teaspoon almond extract
1 cup heavy cream

Combine milk, Cream of Wheat, butter, sugar and salt in a saucepan; cook, stirring constantly until mixture comes to a boil. Cover, lower heat, and cook until very thick, stirring frequently. Divide mixture among 4 dessert dishes, placing pears on top. Spoon apricot jam on top of pears, and trickle Melba sauce over jam. Sprinkle with slivered almonds and pour a little heavy cream over. Serves 4.

`Mr B's Cocktail

Pour the Dubonnet and dry vermouth into a mixing glass half-filled with ice cubes. Stir well. Strain into a cocktail glass, garnish with a lemon twist, and serve in cocktail glass without further garnish. Ingredients: 3 parts Dubonnet, 1 part dry vermouth.

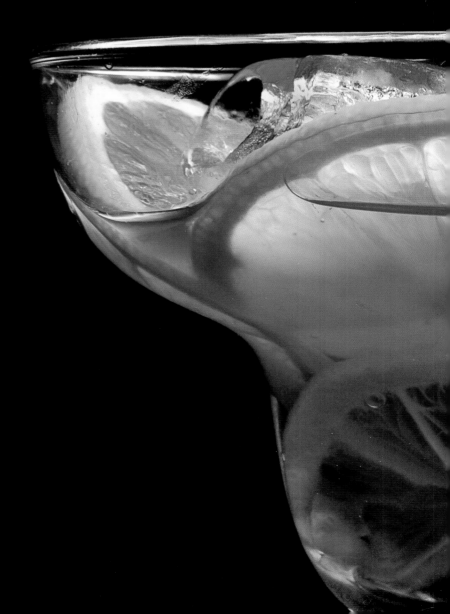

"No matter what he does, he must not rush, yet he must not be late, and the finished product must be exquisite. You need patience, and finally you have to appease your public's appetite. Besides this, it should be inexpensive enough to be accessible, and in itself, the whole must be pretty and there must be a lot of it." That's how Balanchine defined a true cook.

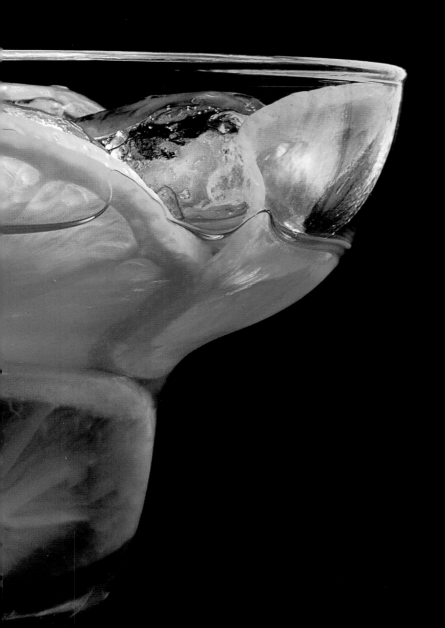

Gogi is the Gimmick at Larue

Early each evening except Mondays, Georgi Tchitchinadze puts on his work clothes in his smart fifteenth-floor apartment at Park Avenue and East Fifty-eighth Street in New York City. He is a graceful, well-built man in his middle forties... simply known as "Gogi," a diminutive of Georgi, and is a native of Tiflis, Georgia... Gogi's work clothes consist of a dark suit, black shoes, a white silk shirt, a plain white four-in-hand tie (his own idea, and a frown for anyone else he catches wearing one), a white carnation and a heady splashing of Chanel No. 5 toilet water.

At 7:30 pm, Tchitchinadze descends to the lobby and walks through a door into Gogi's Larue, the newest sensation among elegant New York dine-and-dance joints. And now Gogi, the Man with the Delicate Air, and the favorite host and intimate of the champagne-and-truffles set in New York, Hollywood, Paris and Mexico City, is ready for the night's work...

Gogi is autocrat, greeter, social arbiter and psychological bouncer of Larue. He welcomes princes and merchants, dowagers and dizzy blondes with the vast charm which is his stock in trade. He assigns tables according to a form chart he carries in his head. And he brushes off undesirables with an instant and almost imperceptible switch from warmth to deep freeze.

Until Gogi took over Larue in November, 1950, it was just another nice stop on the fashionable East Side cafe circuit. But when it became Gogi's Larue, a minor miracle was wrought. Overnight, the club became the rendezvous of the "names" of Park Avenue, Wall Street, Hollywood, Broadway, café society, international society and the business

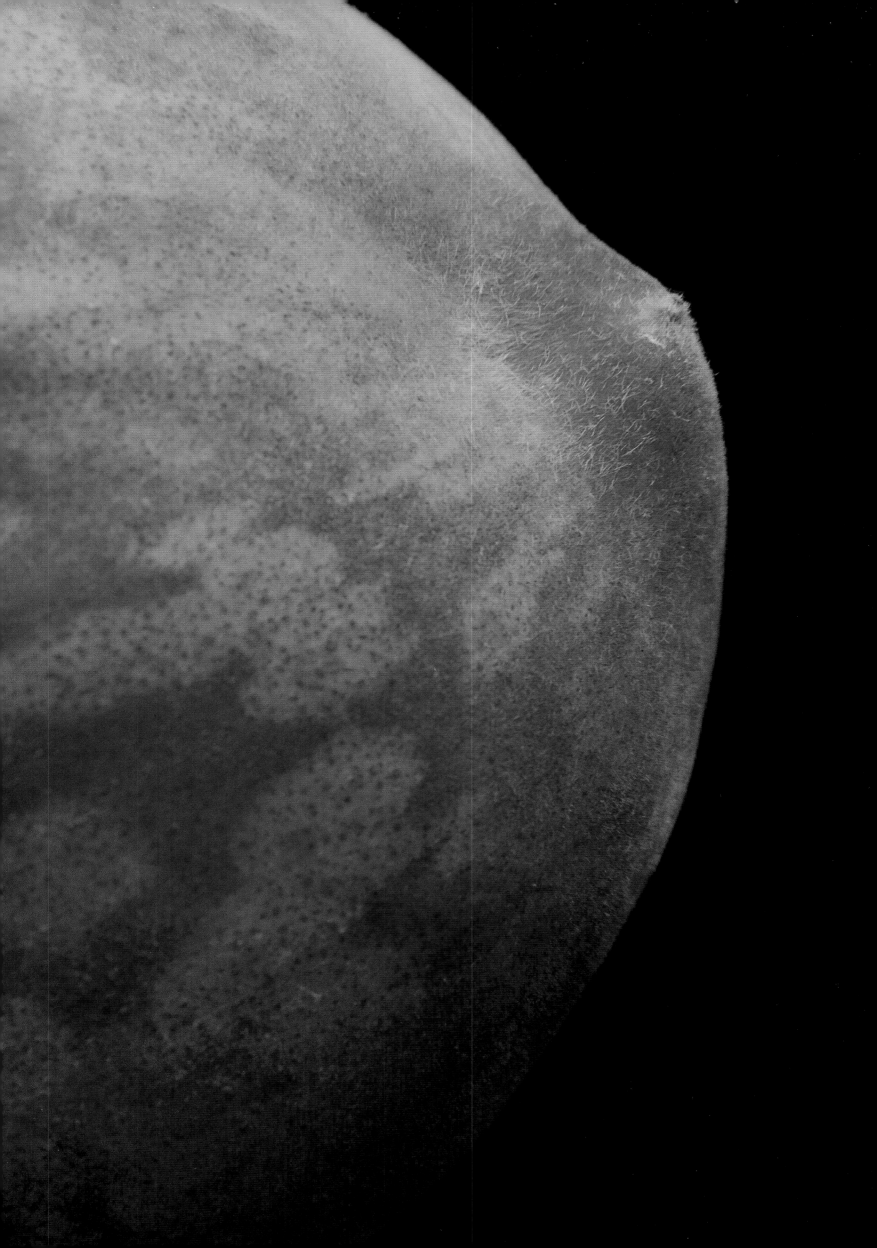

"At 7:30 pm, Tchitchinadze descends to the lobby and walks through a door into Gogi's Larue, the newest sensation among elegant New York dine-and-dance joints. Overnight, the club became the rendezvous of the "names" of Park Avenue, Wall Street, Hollywood, Broadway, cafe society, international society and the business world."

world. It has become the headquarters of movie stars visiting New York... Princes and princesses, dukes and duchesses rub shoulders at Larue with garment tycoons, models, moneyed out-of-towners and celebrity hungry tourists...

A couple of years ago, Gogi was manager of a fashionable spot on the East Side called the Barberry Room. It was a great success, but Gogi was dissatisfied; he yearned for a place of his own. Then he spotted Larue, which was for sale, and immediately sought out his good friend, Manhattan attorney A. Edward Masters, and announced that he wanted to buy the place.

"Fine," Masters said. "How about the money?"

"I haven't got the money," Gogi said. "But I have the friends."

Gogi thereupon started canvassing his close acquaintances in New York, where he had spent two years, and in Hollywood, where he had spent almost 12.

As a result of his efforts, he soon had some of the prettiest partners a man could want (as well as some with the prettiest bank rolls) and he also had $130,000. Among his backers... are Hedy Lamarr and Joan Crawford; Mrs. Emmy Burlingham and Mrs. Sophie Gimbel of New York society; Cornel Wilde, Tony Martin and Bing Crosby; hotel men Conrad Hilton, Joe Drown and Michael Gottlieb; merchants Nathan and Jerry Ohrbach; Hubie Boscowitz, Herbie Klotz, Horace Schmidlapp, and Baron Polan, all men about town, and Jack Barry, radio and television producer-performer... The deal was they get a half ownership in Larue and Gogi owns the rest...

The redecoration of the club was directed by Dick Kollmar, actor and husband of Dorothy Kilgallen, Broadway columnist for the New York Journal-American... The main room, which has the dance floor, seats 200, and is done in pink and black. The other room is called the Plush Room, and it's Gogi's pride and joy: luxurious and soundproofed, seating 52, and done in Napoleonic decor with red velvet walls, gold and white trim, and crystal. Music in the Plush Room is supplied by George Fejer, pianist, who remembers some 1,800 songs. It is a room over whose clientele Gogi does his most careful thinking. He's a one-man board of admission.

When Margaret Truman entered the Plush Room for the first time, she murmured: "Isn't it a shame Daddy never gets to see such beautiful things as this?" This quote is revered by Gogi and, of course, by Kollmar...

A sampling of the crowd at Gogi's on a recent weekday night showed these present: Georgian Prince Dimitri Djordjadze, the noted horseman; actresses Sarah Churchill, Jennifer Jones and Ginger Rogers; Winthrop Rockefeller; actors Ricardo Cortez and Bert Lahr; singers Tony Martin and Johnny Johnston and movie producer David O. Selznick – besides such partners as Jack Barry and Nathan Ohrbach. The Duchess of Windsor is a frequent guest, as are numerous other folk with titles attached to their names.

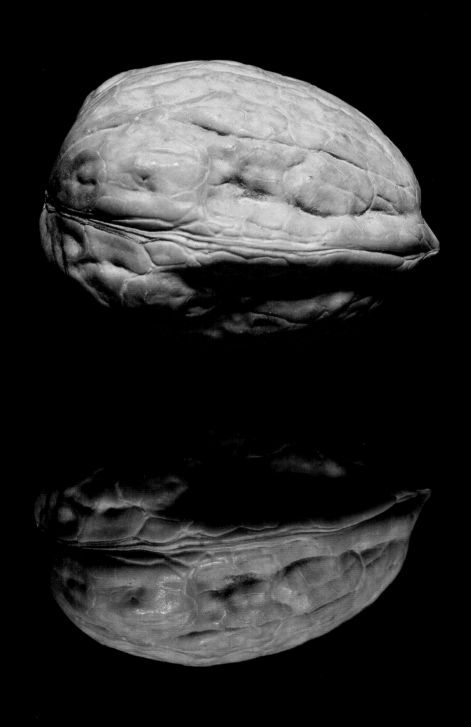

Dress is informal at Larue, except at the brilliant dress galas Gogi throws on the last Thursday of each month. At these affairs, the ladies often are loaded down with as much as $2,000,000 in jewels, furs and gowns, by rough estimate. At one gala, Hope Hampton, widow of financier Jules Brulatour, alone wore $150,000 worth of sparklers, give or take a lavaliere.

As befits a man who operates in such awesome circles, Gogi talks in a soft, soothing voice. He speaks five languages – his native Georgian, Russian, French, Spanish and English. His English is piquant – cultured, yet faintly accented and prone to trouble with verb forms and other obstacles – he calls his wife, the Hollywood beauty Janet Thomas, "the Janet"...

Night-club savants agree that Gogi is the gimmick at Larue, the big difference between just another club and a smash hit. And typical of the things which set him apart is that he's the only cafe host in New York – and you can include Des Moines, too – who greets Madam with a bow and a kiss of the hand...

"You may kiss the lady's hand," Gogi says, "only under two conditions. Wan, she must be the old friend. Two, she must be married. In these cases, the kiss on the hand is the sign of the utmost respect. Wan should never kiss the hand of the unmarried lady."

Gogi also discloses that a little cheating goes on in the hand-kissing department. "It's not be necessary to actually kiss the hand," he explains. "You can hold on the lady's hand and kiss your own."

Gogi's greeting for his close men friends is in the European fashion – a bear hug or a tight squeeze of the arms with the hands. A Gogi squeeze is a substantial affair, for the Man with the Delicate Air is an ex-athlete and a solidly muscled citizen despite his night-club pallor and his penchant for toilet water...

Gogi's rule for judging the class of strangers who come a-knocking at the glass doors at Larue is a simple one: "Always size up the woman. If she's dressed in good taste, let them in. Never look at the man. He could look like the bum and be the gentleman. And vice versa."

Once inside, the patrons find their host truly impressive, judging from available comment. Broadway columnist Louis Sobol says of Gogi, "He's terrifically solicitous. Other night-club hosts worry about your food and the service. Gogi goes further, if he knows you. He worries about you away from the club."...

"Gogi is the only 'gentleman host' in the business," says Hubie Boscowitz. "He has the uncanny knack of knowing when to visit with his patrons and, more important, when to stay away."

There are endless opportunities for worry in running a smart night club, and the Duchess of Windsor... figured in a couple of these genteel rhubarbs.

The Merry Wife of Windsor had always seemed to enjoy herself at Larue, whether it's for a quiet meal or impromptu singing with Ethel Merman... But came the night of the trouble. The duchess was at her favorite table... by the ultra chic Plush Room... when she snapped at Gogi:

"I see you do not wish me to come here any more." Gogi was wounded. How could she say such a thing?

"The lights," the duchess said. "They are bright tonight. I will not come here any more." And she swept out.

"The duchess," Gogi explains, "likes the very dim lighting. Usually, she has it here, but I am noticing the other people they get sleepy and call for their checks when the lights are so low. So this night, I have the lights turned up little bit. The duchess notices this, and she gets angry. But what could I do?"

Happily, the duchess recanted and did visit Larue again...

The chef at Larue is Fernand Desbans. A peppery little Frenchman... who was once chef for the late Prince Louis II of Monaco... He makes special notes about the moneyed munchers who have definite ideas on how their food is to be served. The Duchess of Windsor goes for one lamb chop, and it must be trimmed. Everett Crosby, Bing's brother, fancies the saddle of deer and a soufflé harlequin. Billy Seeman, the big canned-food man, fancies veal cooked in paper. Georgian Prince Gourielli, who has a perfume named after him, is an expert on shashlik and Bordeaux wines. Man about town Count Vasilli (Vava) Adlerberg goes for the Kiev cutlets (breaded veal and chicken).

Besides the excellence of its cuisine, Larue has numerous other claims to distinction. One is that it's the only restaurant with a real prince for a night steward. He's Prince David ("Dolik," they call him affectionately) Vatchnadze, a gentle little representative of czarist royalty whom Gogi knew as a boy in Georgia. It's only at greeting and parting that Dolik's regal bearing pops out from among the cabbages and veal kidneys. He seems to grow in stature as he stands stiffly erect, elbows turned out, clicks his heels, and bows. The prince and Gogi are both refugees from Bolshevism.

Gogi's night-club experience goes back to 1925, when he and three other "émigrés" opened the *Casanova* in Paris. He had come to Paris a few years earlier from Tiflis, and had engaged in various pursuits before finding his true medium: he had put in a few years at the Sorbonne; played professional soccer; danced professionally in Caucasian costume, complete with astrakhan hat and dagger; and had sold "the champagne." The *Casanova* was a success, and was followed by two other Paris night-club ventures, the *Monseigneur* and *Don Juan*. It was at this stage that Gogi laid the foundation of the tremendous pyramid of friendship he has built among the titled and moneyed. Among his pals were international playboys like the late Freddy

"My first picture," he recalls, "was with Bing Crosby. Honeymoon in Paris. I am the French count. They give me 10 pages dialogue. I have so much trouble, they keep cutting, and finally, I got only two lines left, 'Hello, everybody,' and 'Goodbye, everybody.'"

McEvoy, recently drowned aboard his yacht; Baron Pantz, and Baron Nicki Ginzberg. In the early 1930s. Gogi set out for America, with Hollywood as his destination. He learned English by sitting through countless movies. It was the era of the Jimmy Cagney-type film, and some of the first expressions Gogi learned were, "Aw-right, you guys ..." and for repartee, "Oh, yeah?" Among Gogi's first friends in Hollywood was Everett Crosby, who had the idea of making a movie actor out of Gogi. The results apparently support Gogi's statement that he was the worst movie actor in history. Like all Gaul, Gogi's career was divided into three parts – Paramount, Universal and Monogram.

"My first picture," he recalls, "was with Bing Crosby. Honeymoon in Paris. I am the French count. They give me 10 pages dialogue. I have so much trouble, they keep cutting, and finally, I got only two lines left, 'Hello, everybody,' and 'Good-bye, everybody.'

"Next, I am in Alias the Dickens, with Bob Burns and Mischa Auer. I am the French barber, and I am suppose to run in the saloon and scream. 'Oil is discover!' in French. I like this because I can speak the French. So what happens? 1 cannot scream, not even in the French. The voice is gone.

"Last stop, Monogram. I am the gangster. I got lines like, 'Donja nobody move!' I am suppose to kill three people, real tough guy. But I got to keep saying lots of lines before I kill them, and I have the trouble. So the director says: 'I got idea. We are losing time with this bum. Get him out of the way fast.' So instead of me killing three people, they kill me right away, soon as the picture starts. So then I know this acting business is not for me."

Broderick Crawford, Franchot Tone and Auer then backed Gogi in a night club called the *Scheherazade* and again he had a winner, meanwhile increasing his circle of friends in the movie capital. From Hollywood, the restless Georgian lit out for Mexico City. Here he opened a tremendously successful night club, *Ciro's*, with A.C. (Blumey) Blumenthal, who had been a pal of New York's Mayor Jimmy Walker...

Gogi also fought a bull at Cuernavaca on a bet. In prize-fight lingo, he win, but not easy.

"I take the lessons from Silvio Perez, he is the top bullfighter, for two weeks," Gogi recalls. "Then I fight the bull. I am so scare, my hands are shaking, and first time I make the pass, the sword flies out of the hand. It is very embarrassing, because I go to look for the sword and the bull goes with me. Finally, I get him. To tell the truth, I am not much of the bullfighter – and he is not much of the bull."

Gogi finally left Mexico City and returned to Hollywood, where he managed the *Mocambo* and then the *Bel-Air Hotel*. Straeter was leading the orchestra at the hotel at the time and was impressed by Gogi's magic way with a room...

Gogi's first New York venture was managing the *Barberry Room*, and he scored again. It became popular with a widely varied clientele, from Phil Rizzuto of the Yankees to some of Gogi's titled friends... His diversions include bridge, at which he yearns to be a champion, tennis out-doors with Kollmar and Barry, the theatre with his wife on Monday, his night off – and Baseball...

Late in the afternoon before the reopening of Larue last September, Gogi and Kollmar gave the exquisite Plush Room a final look. Everything appeared in perfect order. Yet there was one flaw... "That cash register on the bar," he said. "Everything else is beautiful red and gold, and look at it!"...

They rustled up some paint – and gilded the till.

With this step, Gogi's Larue, in the estimation of its admirers, carved itself a special niche among the posh spots of Manhattan. Obviously, the answer to "How chic can you get?" is the golden dinger on the Plush Room bar at Larue.

Murray Robinson,
Collier's Weekly
1952

"Obviously, the answer to "How chic can you get?" is the golden dinger on the Plush Room bar at Larue."

The Mdivanis

Alexis, David , Serge, Roussadana and Nina Mdivani

Georgian-born American and European public figures of Café Society, the Mdivani siblings were also known as the "Marrying Mdivanis". Louise Astor Van Alen, a member of the Astor and Vanderbilt families, Barbara Hutton, the richest woman at the time (the Woolworth heiress), Mistinguett and the movie legend Pola Negri, opera star Mary McCormic, silent film star Mae Murray and Sinclair Oil heiress, Virginia Sinclair; no one could resist the charms of Alexis, Serge and David Mdivani.

Their sister Nina Mdivani married Denis Conan Doyle, a son of Sir Arthur Conan Doyle, the creator of Sherlock Holmes. Roussadana Mdivani, a sculptor, married the Spanish painter Jose Maria Sert, famous for his murals at the Waldorf Astoria NYC and 30 Rockefeller Center.

In order to understand the effect Alexis would produce on all the girls, one has to place him in the context of the 1920s. Girls had shortened their skirts and dreamed only of flirting and fox-trot. In this context, the crude and frivolous charm of Alexis made it work all the time. He was the God of the beach, the ace of Polo and the idol of the tea dances. No girl could resist him.

Polo represented his only real occupation. He and his brothers were champions. Alexis, who exceeded his brothers, claimed himself as the best player of his generation. Maharajahs contended for the honour of playing against him. So did aristocrats. He played on the team of Lord Mountbatten."

Francis Dorleans,
Snob Society

Chicken Chakhokhbili

Also known as "Prince Mdivani Special"

2 small chickens
½ cup butter
1 onion, sliced
1/3 cup sherry
½ cup tomato juice
1 cup water
1 teaspoon paprika
1 teaspoon salt
Pepper

Cut the chicken into quarters; then rinse the pieces and pat them dry. Melt the butter in a frying pan and fry the chicken until light brown. Remove the chicken to a baking pan, leaving the dripping in the frying pan. Fry the onion in the dripping until soft and golden, then pour over the chicken. Add the remaining ingredients. Bake uncovered in a hot oven (200°C/400°F) for one hour, turning the chicken over after the first half hour. The juices in the pan make a delicious gravy. Serve with rice. Makes 8 servings.

"They understand the art of flattery as do no other men I have ever met. And the art of flattery is almost a lost one in this realistic and humourless age. That, I assure you, is the secret of the Mdivani charm for women, I know."

Pola Negri - Hollywood actress and femme fatale

George Papashvily

Georgian-American writer and sculptor. Together with his wife Helen Waite he wrote several best-sellers often based on his experiences as a penniless immigrant and his culinary memoirs of Georgia. His book, *Anything can Happen*, was made into a Hollywood film in 1952.

"On the eighth day of Creation, God divided men into nations and told them to select a place for their country. After everyone was satisfied and had settled down, God started home. On the way, He passed the Georgians who were sitting around a table in an arbour by the roadside.

God scolded them. 'While you sat here eating and drinking, singing and joking, the whole world was divided up. Now nothing is left for you.'

The Tamada, as we call the head of the table, apologized. 'It was very wrong, we know. But God, while we enjoyed ourselves we didn't forget you. We drank to You to thank You for making such a beautiful world.'

'That's more than anybody else did.' God said, 'So I'm going to give you the last little corner of the earth – the place I was saving for myself because it is most like Paradise.'

Two parts of the story at least are true. Georgians do spend hours around the table, not just for food and drink, but also to enjoy the company of their friends."

George Papashvily

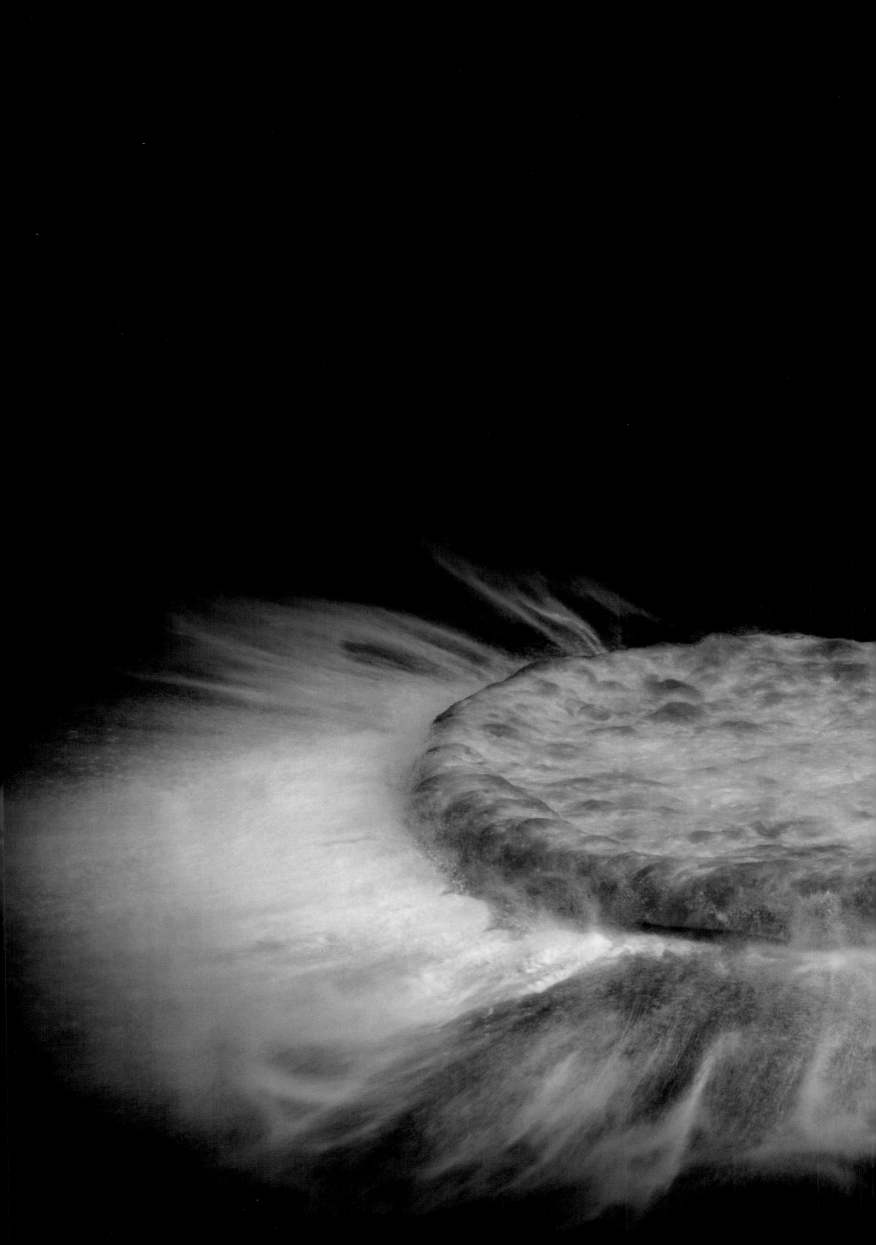

Khachapuri

Perfectly round, golden brown like a midday sun or lightly dusted with flour, Khachapuri is the most famous of all Georgian dishes. Each region has its own variation, but everywhere it remains the most familiar and welcoming dish. No 'supra' is complete without it.

Khachapuri

Dough

2 packages active dry yeast
½ teaspoon plus 1 tablespoon sugar
1 cup lukewarm milk (43°C/110°F to 46°C/115°F)
3½ to 4 cups all-purpose flour
2 teaspoons salt
8 tablespoons butter, softened (¼-pound stick)

Filling:

900g/2 pounds sweet Muenster cheese,
finely grated by hand or in a blender
2 tablespoons butter, softened
1 egg
1 egg, lightly beaten (for tarts)
2 tablespoons finely chopped coriander

Sprinkle the 2 packages of yeast and the ½ teaspoon of the sugar over ½ cup of lukewarm milk in small, shallow bowl. Set aside for 2 or 3 minutes, then stir until the yeast is thoroughly dissolved. Place in a warm, draft-free spot (such as an unlit oven) for 5 to 8 minutes, or until the mixture has doubled in volume.

Pour 3 cups of the flour into a large mixing bowl and make a deep well in the centre. Add the remaining ½ cup of milk, the yeast mixture, the remaining 1 tablespoon of sugar, 2 teaspoons of salt and 8 tablespoons of butter. With a large spoon, slowly beat the flour into these ingredients and continue to beat vigorously until smooth. Gather the dough into a ball and place it on a lightly floured surface.

Knead the dough by folding it end to end, then pressing it down, pushing it forward with the heel of your hands and folding it back. Knead in this fashion for at least 10 minutes, sprinkling the dough every few minutes with a small handful of as much of the remaining flour as you need to prevent it from sticking to the board.

When the dough is smooth and elastic, place it in a large, lightly buttered bowl. Dust the dough lightly with flour and cover the bowl loosely with a kitchen towel. Let the dough rise in a warm, draft-free place for about 45 minutes to an hour, or until it has doubled in bulk and springs back slowly when gently poked with a finger. Then punch the dough down with a blow of your first and set aside again to rise for another 30 to 40 minutes or until it again doubles in bulk.

softened butter and the whole egg. Beat vigorously with a large spoon until smooth, then purée in a food mill or rub with the back of the spoon through a fine sieve set over a large bowl.

Preheat the oven to 190°C/375°F. To make the round loaf, punch the dough down with a sharp blow of your fist, then roll it on a lightly floured surface into a circle about 58cm/23 inches in diameter.

Use the dough to line a buttered layer-cake tin 23cm/9 inches round by 4cm/1½ inches deep. Then fill it with the cheese mixture, and fold in the ends of dough. Set the loaf aside to rest for 10 to 15 minutes, then bake the bread in the centre of the oven for 1 hour, or until golden brown. Turn the bread out onto a wire cake rack and cool a little before serving.

To make individual tarts, roll the dough into a 60cm/24-inch diameter circle and with an 11cm/4½-inch cookie cutter, cut out 48 rounds. Fill and shape the rounds. Set them side by side on buttered cookie sheets and brush the dough with lightly beaten egg. Let the tarts rest for 10 minutes, then bake them in the centre of the oven for 20 to 25 minutes, or until golden brown. With a wide spatula, transfer the tarts to a serving platter, sprinkle with chopped coriander if desired, and serve warm.

"One can even eat nails with Tkemali"

Nikita Khrushchev

Tkemali

To make 1½ cups:
2 cups water
225 g/½ pound sour plums (about 24)
1 clove garlic, peeled
3 tablespoons finely chopped coriander
¼ teaspoon salt
⅛ teaspoon cayenne pepper
2 tablespoon strained fresh lemon juice

Bring the 2 cups of water to a boil in a medium-sized saucepan and drop in the plums. Remove from the heat and set aside for 10 minutes, then bring the water back to a boil over high heat. Cook briskly uncovered for 10 to 15 minutes, or until the plums are tender. Pour the contents of the pan into a sieve set over a small bowl and set the liquid aside.

With a small, sharp knife cut out and discard the plum pits and combine the plums, garlic and coriander in an electric blender. Pour in ¼ cup of the reserved plum liquid and blend at high speed, gradually adding the remaining plum liquid. The blended sauce should have the consistency of sour cream.

With a rubber spatula, transfer the sauce to a larger saucepan and stir in the salt and pepper. Bring to a boil over high heat, then, off the heat, stir the lemon juice. Cool to room temperature and serve with shashlyk or tabaka.

"I would not be surprised," a chef once told George Papashvily, "to learn that Georgians eat sauce on sauce"

Bright red or deep velvet violet, green asparagus or autumn-leaf yellow, the sauces in Georgian cuisine not only bring in touches of joyful colour but enhance each dish with their bold bouquets of spices mixed with fruits. The most famous of them is Tkemali, the sour plum sauce.

Once, a group of Indians on horses rescued Papashvily's truck from the river, and to thank them he decided to cook: "Now, I'd like to invite all you boys to a party. I cook you a sheep how we do it in my country"

While little Indian boys made the fire, Papashvily prepared the sheep, cut wooden spits, and skewered the meat. After two hours Shashlyk was ready. He started with the old Indian headman and passed a good smoking hot stickful of meat to everyone, in the order of what he guessed their ages might be.

A young English-speaking Indian said: "My grandfather likes the way you kill sheep and clean and cook. He wants to know what tribe you come from. How many sheep you have? Is good hunting there?"

"I'm Georgian," Papashvily answered, "from the other side of the world. In our village was about two hundred sheep last time I knew. If we kill with care, our hunting is enough for all."

To thank him in return, the young Indian gave Papashvily a little piece of stone, and as George didn't have much left except a combination corkscrew knife, he made him present of that.

"These guys know how to act like men" Papashvily said to himself, "and they do." They shook hands, and they all rode away.

Shashlyk "Mtsvadi"

Shashlik "Mtsvadi"

To Serve 4
1 large onion, peeled and finely grated
1 tablespoon strained fresh lemon juice
1 tablespoon olive oil
1 teaspoon salt
¼ teaspoon freshly ground black pepper
1.8 kilos/2 pounds boneless leg or shoulder of
lamb, trimmed of excess fat and cut into
2.5cm/1 to 4cm/1½ inch cubes
2 medium onions, cut into 0.6cm/¼-inch-thick
chunks

Garnish
2 medium firm, ripe tomatoes, cut into
eights
10 scallions, trimmed
1 lemon, quartered

In a large mixing bowl, beat together the grated onion, lemon juice, olive oil, salt and pepper. Add the meat and let it marinate for at least 3 hours at room temperature, tossing it about in the marinade every hour or so to keep the pieces well moistened.

Light a layer of coals in a charcoal grill and burn until a white ash appears on the surface, or preheat your kitchen grill to its highest point.

String the cubes of lamb tightly on 4 long skewers, alternating the lamb with the chunks of onion; press them firmly together. Grill 10cm/4 inches from the source of heat, turning the skewers occasionally, until the lamb is done to your taste and the onions are brown. For pink lamb, allow about 10 minutes; for well-done lamb, more typical of Georgian cooking, allow about 15 minutes. Slide the lamb and onions off the skewers on to heated individual plates, and serve with the raw tomatoes and scallions.

Khinkali

Freshly emigrated to the United States, George Papashvily and his friends were looking to start a business to make them rich.

"In America what's everybody doing all the time – asked Vallodia –"Eating! If they're not eating they're chewing on gum to fool themselves they're eating. Cook some kind of food and sell. Make big money."

But what to cook? They thought and thought and finally decided on khinkali. A test batch was prepared to sell to restaurants. After a few refusals, he finally came to a Greek. He tasted.

"O.K.," he said, "I'm gonna take fifty dozen for trial because tonight I have banquet party. You be here sure six o'clock with khinkali. Not one minute late"

After a few misadventures on the way to the bakery to buy dough, which was almost six miles away, the clock struck five before he got home. Running out of time Papashvily hollered to the neighbors. "Come on up and help make khinkali or we not gonna get finished."

Up they came and they started: Anna rolled. Vallodia and George portioned meat. Luba pinched. Ahmed and Hassan kept new water boiling. Madame Greskin counted out dozens. His Excellency packed. Artash ran up and down and shoved boxes on the borrowed truck.

Ten minutes to six they finished. Papashvily delivered khinkali and earned his forty dollars. "Now we figure the profit – For meat was $10, dough $3", "$10 on trolley", Papashvily counted, "and I bought $4 of wine for the boys. But can't give bottle of wine to an admiral from Imperial Russian Navy, so I bought him cognac instead. $6".

"Can't give daughter of admiral no bottle wine neither so that roses with sincere compliments. $6…

"and truck, gas, kids Luba and Artash to movies in loge seats…."

With $1.67 profit, Vallodia thought awhile. "You excuse me now, I gonna speak to you from the heart like a friend. You're no man for business George. You hafta look your luck some other place."

Khinkali

Beef
Onions
Herbs
Salt, pepper, water

For khinkali you take fresh bright beef piece, chop fine, cut onions and herbs over; put pepper, little; salt, little more again; water; and mix all. Then you roll a nice dough thin as oak leaf, put the meat in, pinch the edges all around and drop one by one into pot of boiling water and when the water is boiling, it's done.

You take out, bite a hole in the end, drink the juice and eat the meat and its coat. Ten, twenty – with good appetite man can eat thirty. That's khinkali.

Extracted from George Papashviliys book ,

'*Anything can Happen.*'

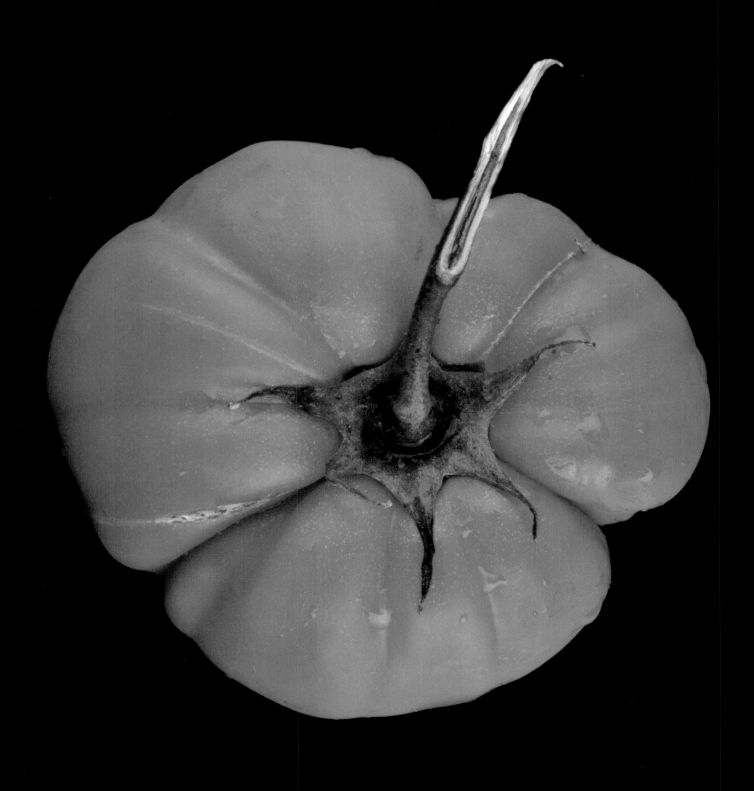

In the run up to his wedding to Helena, George Papashvily asked his fellow Georgian émigré friend, Uncle John who was an excellent cook, to prepare the wedding dinner. After the ceremony, Uncle John took the newlywed bride aside to share a secret.

"What did Uncle John told you?" Papashvily could not resist the curiosity.

Helena's laughing. "Another recipe"

"My God, what was this one for?"

"If you want to be happy married," he whispered in my ear, "at least once a day say to your husband, 'I love you!' and whenever you set a table for Georgians, remember – only too much is ever enough."

Tamara Toumanova

Tamara Toumanova (Toumanishvili), also known as "the Black Pearl" of the Russian Ballet, made her debut aged six at the Trocadéro de Paris. As one of the 'Baby Ballerinas' of the Ballets Russes de Monte Carlo at 13, by her late teens she had become an international phenomenon. Her dark dramatic beauty would inspire the likes of George Balanchine, Jean Cocteau, Serge Lifar, Gene Kelly and Alfred Hitchcock.

Tamara Toumanova, although descended from Georgian nobility (the Toumanishvili and Chkheidze families), was born in a train goods wagon in Siberia as her mother fled the communist revolution.

From a very early age she began to study ballet and under the personal tutelage of Balanchine himself.

"When Balanchine came I could feel his electrifying greatness. Preobrajenska asked me to do the most difficult technical movements and I did everything, and then of course there was my personality."

He told her "I will take you with me, and I will do the best possible."

"He took care of me", Tamara recalled, "he used to tell Mama what to do, what food to give me, not to overdo!... I really think that Balanchine looked upon me as his own child. He would play with me." She thought he felt a kindship with her "with my *tristesse*, with my being part Georgian."

Fillet de Sole Véronique

4-6 fillets of sole
Salt and pepper
1½ cups white wine
½ teaspoon onion juice
225g/½ pound seedless grapes
¼ lb. butter
6 tablespoons flour
1 cup chicken bouillon

Place fish in greased baking dish; sprinkle lightly with salt and pepper. Pour wine and onion juice over fish. Bake at 170°C/325°F for 5 minutes; add grapes to baking dish and cover loosely with waxed paper. Bake another 15 minutes; remove paper, pour off fish liquid and reserve. Turn off oven heat; keep fish warm in oven.

Melt butter, add flour, cook over low heat 1 minute. Remove from heat; blend in reserved fish liquid and chicken bouillon. Return to heat, and bring to a boil stirring constantly. Cook 2 minutes or until thick. Pour sauce over fish and serve with tiny, sweet, peas. Serves 4-6.

"The start of Tamara's relationship with the legendary ballerina Anna Pavlova was somewhat amusing. During a school rehearsal in 1925, Tamara's mother Eugenia, known as the famous "Ballet Mother", was standing next to the Anna Pavlova. Whilst admiring her beloved daughter's performance, she exclaimed "My Tamara is the best!", to which Pavlova responded with modest commendation. Offended by the lack of enthusiasm, Eugenia failing to recognise the renowned ballerina asked "Do you dance yourself?". "Just a little bit" responded Pavlova. After this rehearsal a select few were picked from Preobrajenska's school for Pavlova's gala concert at Trocadéro de Paris, Tamara was one of them."

Olga Stark, Monte-Carlo Ballet principal ballerina

Poulet au Jus d'Orange

1 frying chicken, cut in pieces
Salt and pepper
3 tablespoons sweet butter
¾ cup orange juice concentrate
½ cup water

Sprinkle chicken with salt and pepper. Melt butter in a skillet; brown chicken on all sides. Add orange juice concentrate and water; cover and simmer, turning frequently, until chicken is tender, about 30 minutes. Serve over green beans with boiled rice; Serves 2-4.

Three very young girls with amazing technical proficiency gained great fame as the "Baby Ballerinas" of the Ballet Russe de Monte Carlo. They were variously known to be twelve, thirteen, fourteen or fifteen – take your pick. As the English dancer Diana Gould, who was in the company, was to comment, "I can't remember how many times we celebrated Toumanova's fifteenth birthday."

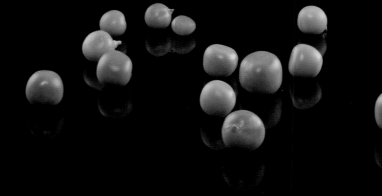

Bifteck aux Champignons à la Crème

4 cube steaks 0.6cm/¼ inch thick
Salt and pepper
2 tablespoons butter
225g/¼ pound mushrooms, sliced
1 cup sour cream

Season steaks with salt and pepper. Melt butter in a heavy skillet, brown steaks quickly on both sides. Remove steaks and set aside. Sauté sliced mushrooms in pan and add sour cream; bring to simmering, stirring constantly; add steaks and heat. Serve with rice to which raisins, plumped in boiling water, have been added. Serves 4.

"Balanchine once recalled: 'Toumanova, you know, had wonderful balance. She practiced all the time. She stood like this' (he sketches in a pose on pointe); 'her mother brought her lunch while she stood. It was in France; she got paid in cash and she signed, balancing.' He mimes taking an envelope and signing the receipt while on one foot. 'So in *Le Baiser de la Fée*, I made a passage for her in which she stands on one foot, looking for him.' He shades his eyes with his hand, looking into the distance. 'In rehearsals, it was fine; she stood there forever. In dress rehearsal, she stood. Opening night, the curtain went up and – she fell. This is the way it happens'."

Joseph H. Mazo
Dance is a Contact Sport

Prince Nicholas Toumanoff

Prince "Nicky" Toumanoff (the Russification of the Georgian name Toumanishvili), as he was better known, was a celebrated backgammon champion and 'personality' in American high society. He became one of the leading promoters of the sport in the US. Aside from his Caucasian passion for backgammon, he was an enthusiastic gourmet and a socialite.

He stepped out with the likes of Jean Nash Dubonnet and married the famous couturier Marusia Toumanoff Sassi, who regularly collaborated with Travis Banton, the chief designer at Paramount Pictures. Her designs were worn by Rosalind Russell, Greer Garson and Doris Day, among many others.

> "Bachelor of the Week today is Prince Nicholas Toumanoff. He divides his time between his homes in California, New York and Florida. He is an enthusiastic gourmet, who has sampled the great foods of the great homes and great restaurants of the world."
>
> *Palm Beach Daily News*

Nicky's Fizz

Special for Prince Toumanoff

by Franz Meier of the Hemingway Bar, Hotel Ritz, Paris

In shaker: one half glass of sweetened grapefruit juice, one glass of gin (approx 100gms). Shake well, strain into fizz glass add Schweppes, soda water or syphon and serve.

How I discovered Tamadism

"For a long time, Georgia was just a gaping wound for me. My mother, who was born in the Aragvi Valley, had fled the country in the 1930s. Two men were pursuing her: Stalin, who had little appreciation for her freedom of spirit, and Beria, who loved her a little too much. I was therefore born in the heart of the English countryside. But each of the two men suspected the other of being my father and ceaselessly sent their henchmen – even as far as the hallways of Cambridge – to try and kill me. The only reason for me signing up to the British secret services was to try and learn the necessary techniques to save my own life. But my salvation came from philosophy. I shall not expand further here on this life of the spirit, the only worthy life, or on my relationships with Ludwig Wittgenstein, Claude Lévi-Strauss or Ruhollah Khomeiny. One day perhaps I will write the story, the secret epic tale of the past century.

I knew nothing of the land of my ancestors. It was therefore with a feeling of unsettling strangeness that I found myself, one fine day in May 1989, in the narrow streets of the old quarter of Tiflis. The flight that should have taken me from Tehran to Moscow had been interrupted, for technical or mystical reasons, in the socialist republic of Georgia, which was living its last days. The "Iveria" Intourist hotel, in which the airline company had put me without asking my opinion, was already nothing more than a bullet-ridden ghost. People whom I did not know, friends of friends of friends, welcomed me in a way that I had never been welcomed before. This hospitality did not have the slightly hypocritical, standardized taste to which I was accustomed. My hosts couldn't care less that I was the winner of the Nobel Prize for philosophy and the world-famous author of *Ontologie du hasard*. They were very interested in my origins, but I disappointed them

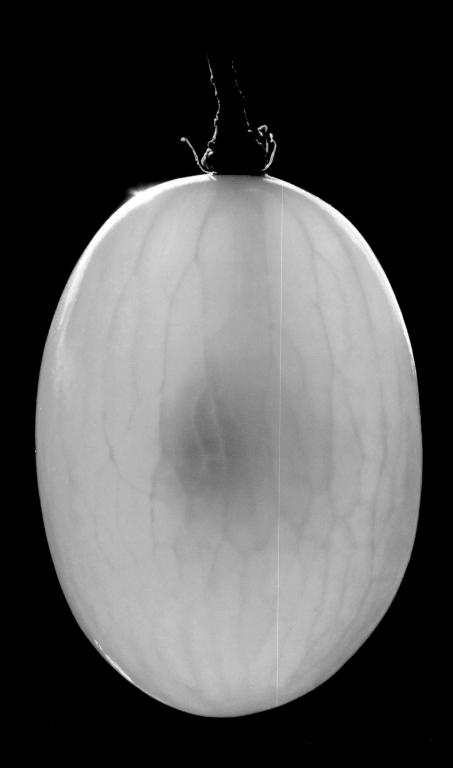

in this area, since my mother had carefully hidden the history of my family and even that of my birth. Despite my ignorance of the Georgian language, they continued to recognize in my face the traits of such and such an acquaintance. In short, they adopted me with an elegant insouciance – the mask of supreme delicacy – that I have never experienced again elsewhere.

But it was an evening in an apartment in the old quarter of Tiflis that left me the most lasting impression. My unknown friends had invited me to dinner. A young, charming couple welcomed me as if I was an old chum. Countless guests glided into a huge room lined with a balcony and cluttered with a vast range of objects, including yellowing posters, a kitsch calendar, a mauve teddy bear and, among the tapestries, icons and shelves of old books in French. I picked up a volume of Essais, wondering what worse affront there could be to the Soviet regime than reading Montaigne rather than Lenin.

I was drawn into the feast, which remains to this day the best of my life. I am well familiar with the Mediterranean and Ottoman cuisine, enjoyed from Syracuse to Aleppo, but why did I find these stuffed aubergines, this cheese with mint, these lamb soups, these giant ravioli, these dishes with multi-coloured herbs, among many other delights, finer than the most complex of gastronomic symphonies? I guessed that my hosts had spent their monthly salary on offering me a proper welcome. Above all, they had transformed this improvised meal into a banquet worthy of that related by Plato. If you remember: Socrates, up to dusk, had drunk obscene quantities of wine, evoking love, without giving into animality or exhaustion. The Georgians surrounding me were drinking just like my philosophy master – to become lighter and not to become heavier. To offer grace to their speech and not to demean it. This celebration of the verb never seemed more evident than when I was listening to the words of the tamada, the person appointed to propose toasts. I thought that in the Soviet Union, they only drank to friendship between peoples. Here, listening to the speech of the tamada, with a raised glass, and drinking the horn of young Georgian wine, was a philosophical act in the highest sense of the word. The master of the ceremony, a man aged around sixty, with a thick bald head – and glasses only slightly less thick – and a face as intense as a Fayum mummy portrait, miraculously brought together thought, speech and joy. This man was called Merab. Only later did I learn – such was the extent to which social vanities were set aside here – that he was the greatest of Georgian thinkers. Mamardachvili, such was his name, was born in Gori like Stalin and symbolically represented the antidote. He had seen the destruction of free thought, stifled in the deadly lexicon of sovietism. He revived it through the verb at a dinner among friends. During his toasts, he evoked Descartes, Proust, Montesquieu or even Marx freed from the intellectual prison of communism. Above all, he spoke about the joy of thinking, of the commitment of the whole being to the search for truth, of this ultimate art which consists, as he put it, of living à propos... I knew the lectures, treaties and symposiums. But I had never heard this before; thinking that is uttered, shared and drunk with friends. Not an authoritarian, bombastic speech, not advertising or business communication, not noncommittal chat, but rather the authentic Logos, which invites us to converse and search for the meaning of the apparently most obvious things. To celebrate language, I knew about praying, love declarations, or even reading. Not the art of proposing toasts.

Our conversations, light and amusing, yet on crucial subjects, carried on until the following morning. And we were only tipsy, as if carried by grace. I then understood that Georgia was bringing Ancient Athens to life. And that it had created, oh, certainly not a school, academy or movement. No, much better than that, it had created a style that gave language its essence back. I call it Tamadism; though that cannot be written. Somewhere in Caucasia, at the height of totalitarianism, thought, speech and life were reinvented. Without forgetting to have fun. Or to drink."

Marcello Yashvili-McGregor Jr,

Courtesy of Michel Eltchaninoff

Salome
Andronikov
(Andronikashvili)

1888-1982

George
Balanchine
(Balanchivadze)

1904 - 1983

Prince and Princess
Peter Bagration
(Bagrationi)

1765-1812

George
Papashvily
(Papashvili)

1898 - 1978

Alexis
Mdivani &
family

1905 - 1935

Tamara
Toumanova
(Toumanishvili)

1919 - 1996

Prince Nicolas
Toumanoff
(Toumanishvili)

1911 - 1992

Acknowledgements

Antonius Moonen, *Petit Breviaire du Snobisme* (French), Editions L'Inventaire , 2010 – Pg. 39

Arthur Gold and Robert Fizdale, *The Gold and Fizdale Cookbook – Food for Good Living*, Random House, New York, October 1984 – Pgs. 42, 44-46, 48, 51, 52, 54, 60, 63, 64, 68-70, 82-74

Beatrice De Holguin, *Wedding Bell Time Sounds in Resort*, Palm Beach Daily News, Palm Beach, Florida, 09 March 1969 – Pg. 120

Francis Dorléans, *Snob Society* © Flammarion, 2009 – Pg. 92

Frank Meier , *The Artistry Of Mixing Drinks* (RITZ Bar Paris), Fryam Press, Paris, 1936 – Pg. 43

George & Helen Waite Papashvily, *Anything Can Happen*, Harper & Brothers Publishers, New York and London, 1945 – Pgs. 94, 98, 99, 191, 102, 104, 105, 106, 109

George Mardikian, *Kitchen Cabinet*, Sunset Publishing Corporation, Menlo Park, CA, 1995 – Pg. 93, recipe

Helen & George Papashvily, *Russian Cooking*, Time Life Books, New York, 1969 – Pgs. 94, 98, 99, 101, 102, 104, 105, 106, 109

Igor Obolensky, *"Судьба красоты. Истории грузинских жен"*, Cezanne Publishing House, Tbilisi, 2010 – Pg. 113

John Steinbeck, *A Russian Journal*, Penguin Books, Harmondsworth. Pgs. 8, 11, 13, 15, 16, 18

Joseph H. Mazo, *Dance is a Contact Sport*, Da Capo Press, Cambridge, MA, 1976 – Pg. 119

Larisa Vasilyeva, *Salomea ili Solominka, ne sognutaya vetrom*, Ogonek Journal No3, 1988 – Pg. 34

Murray Robinson, Collier's Weekly, *Gogi is the Grimick at Larue,* Collier's Magazine, 02 February 1952 – Pgs. 78-89

Robert Gottlieb, George Balanchine: *The Ballet Maker*, Harper Collins Publishers, New York, 2004 – Pg. 111

Robert Talson – *Salomea 1913*, Online publication № 21101281804, www.proza.ru, 2011

Robert Tracy, Sharon DeLano, *Balanchine's ballerinas: conversations with the Muses*, Linden Press/S&S, New York, 1983 – Pg. 110

Salome Andronikov, *Good Food from Abroad (from Caucasus to London via Moscow and Paris)*, The Harvill Press Limited, London, 1953 – Pgs. 22, 24, 25, 32, 33

Tanaquil Le Clercq, *The Ballet Cook Book*, Stein and Day, New York, 1966 – Pgs. 55, 57, 58, 59, 64 (Fast Soup), 65, 67, 74, 77 (Mr B's Sweet Kasha), 112,114, 116

Victor Dandré & Alexandre Vassiliev, *Anna Pavlova: The Life and the Legend*, Vita Nova, St. Petersburg, 2003

Editional Photo Credits

Anna Saldadze: pg. 92

Shutterstock: pgs. 12,39,48,82,86,92,115,116,121,123

Keti Bakradzé

Special acknowledgements to Mrs Keti Bakradzé, head chef at "The Dining Room", Tbilisi, Georgia, for her priceless help and contribution to this book.

Special acknowledgements go also to our families and the people who supported us and participated in the project: Mariam Janashia, Bakur Sulakauri, Tina Mamulashvili and their team, Tamara and Nino Bibilashvili, Mariam Zaldastanishvili, Leila Esaiashvili, Giorgi Tevzadzé, Anna Godabrelidzé, Nato Khurcidzé, Michel Eltchaninof, Victoria Magniant and the Café Angelina in Paris where this project was born.

Anna Saldadze & David Gigauri
Be My Guest - The Georgian recipe for cooking success

Sulakauri Publishing, Tbilisi 2013
© Sulakauri Publishing, 2013

Editors Anna Saldadze & David Gigauri
Photo design by Anna Saldadze, Mariam Janashia
Photography by Mariam Janashia
Food design by Keti Bakradze
Book design by Ia Makhatadze, Giorgi Kevlishvili, Anna Saldadze
Cover design by Natia Kvaratskhelia
Text Editor: Michael Vickers

Very special thanks to Peter Nasmyth

Sulakauri Publishing
David Aghmashenebeli ave. 150, Tbilisi 0112
E-mail: info@sulakauri.ge

ISBN 978-9941-15-879-7
www.sulakauri.ge

Distributed by Mta Publications, London
www.mtapublications.co.uk